Englisch

ABSCHLUSS-PRÜFUNGS-
TRAINER

Hauptschulabschluss
Baden-Württemberg

 scook

AUDIOS
online

Deine **interaktiven Übungen** und **Audios**
findest du auf scook.de. Dort gibst du den unten
stehenden Zugangscode in die Box ein.

rt3vj-7529k

Dein Zugangscode auf
www.scook.de

Die Nutzungsdauer für die Online-Übungen
beträgt nach Aktivierung des Zugangscodes
zwei Jahre. In dieser Zeit speichern wir deine
Lernstandsdaten für dich; nach Ablauf der
Nutzungsdauer werden sie gelöscht.

Cornelsen

Abschlussprüfungstrainer Englisch

Hauptschulabschluss | Baden-Württemberg

Illustrationen:
Cornelsen/Karen Donnelly

Bildquellen:
S. 7 o.: Shutterstock.com/Mike Flippo; **S. 7 u.:** Shutterstock.com/RossHelen; **S. 8:** Shutterstock.com/Jevanto Productions; **S. 9:** Shutterstock.com/Jeff Whyte; **S. 10:** Shutterstock.com/Mikhail Kolesnikov; **S. 12:** akg-images/Science Source; **S. 13:** Shutterstock.com/Constantin Stanciu; **S. 14:** interfoto e.k./Friedrich; **S. 15:** Shutterstock.com/karen roach; **S. 17:** mauritius images/alamy stock photo/Penny Tweedie; **S. 19:** Shutterstock.com/Tukaram.Karve; **S. 21:** Shutterstock.com/Photomika-com; **S. 24:** Shutterstock.com/Boyloso; **S. 26:** Shutterstock.com/Evocation Images; **S. 28:** Shutterstock.com/fizkes; **S. 30:** Shutterstock.com/mubus7; **S. 40:** Shutterstock.com/lkoimages; **S. 45:** Shutterstock.com/Syda Productions; **S. 46:** Shutterstock.com/Elnur; **S. 47 u.:** Shutterstock.com/Vladimir Sviracevic; **S. 48:** Shutterstock.com/Vladimir Sviracevic; **S. 49:** Shutterstock.com/grynold; **S. 50:** Shutterstock.com/valdis torms; **S. 51:** Shutterstock.com/Filipe Frazao

Erarbeitet in der Redaktion von:
Klaus Unger (Projektleitung), Cornelia Frisse (verantwortliche Redakteurin)
sowie Friederike von Bülow, Christine Maxwell, Paulina Schaeffer

Auf der Grundlage von Arbeitsheften folgender Autorinnen und Autoren:
Gwen Berwick, York; Sydney Thorne, York

Beratende Mitwirkung: Tobias Pfeifer, Dossenheim

Layout-Konzept: Klein&Halm Grafikdesign, Berlin
Umschlaggestaltung: Agentur Rosendahl, Berlin
Layout und technische Umsetzung: Andrea Päch (MeGa 14, Berlin)

www.cornelsen.de

1. Auflage, 1. Druck 2020

© 2020 Cornelsen Verlag GmbH, Berlin

Druck: Firmengruppe APPL, aprinta Druck, Wemding

ISBN 978-3-06-035869-4

PEFC zertifiziert
Dieses Produkt stammt aus nachhaltig bewirtschafteten Wäldern und kontrollierten Quellen.
www.pefc.de
PEFC
PEFC/04-32-0928

Inhaltsverzeichnis

VORWORT

TRAINING SECTION

A – Listening comprehension

B – Text-based tasks

C – Use of language

D – Writing

Kommunikationsprüfung

MUSTERPRÜFUNGEN

LÖSUNGEN (als Einleger in der Mitte des Hefts)

Was erwartet dich in der Prüfung?

Die Abschlussprüfung an Hauptschulen in Baden-Württemberg besteht im Fach Englisch aus zwei Prüfungsteilen:

- der **Kommunikationsprüfung**, die von den Lehrerinnen und Lehrern an deiner Schule (nach Vorgaben) entworfen und durchgeführt wird.

- der **schriftlichen Prüfung**, die zentral vom Kultusministerium erstellt wird.

Kompetenz	Aufgaben	Zeit
Teil A: *Listening comprehension* (Hörverstehen)	vier Höraufgaben, verschiedene Formate: · *Multiple choice* (2x) · *Fill in the table* · *Matching*	30 Minuten
15 Minuten Pause		
Teil B: *Text-based tasks* (Leseverstehen)	fünf Aufgaben, verschiedene Formate: · *Multiple choice* (2x) · *Matching* · *True, false, not in the text* · *Find sentences that mean the same*	90 Minuten
Teil C: *Use of language* (Wortschatz, Grammatik)	fünf Aufgaben, verschiedene Formate: · *Fill in the gap / Multiple choice* · *Find the opposites* · *Find the synonyms* · *Give a definition* · *Ask questions*	
Teil D: *Writing* (Schreiben)	zwei Aufgaben: · Korrespondenz (Briefe, E-Mails) zu einer vorgegebenen Situation (60 Wörter) · *Creative writing:* über Erlebnisse, Erfahrungen, Meinungen, Vorlieben schreiben (80 Wörter)	
Kommunikationsprüfung	drei Aufgaben: · Präsentation über ein persönliches Thema · Dialog zu einer vorgegebenen Situation · Sprachmittlung (Mediation): deutsche Informationen/Fragen auf Englisch wiedergeben, englische Informationen/Fragen auf Deutsch	15 Minuten

Themen, Texte und Hilfsmittel in der Prüfung

In der Prüfung wird nicht dein Wissen über ein Thema oder ein Land abgefragt, sondern du sollst zeigen, dass du auf Englisch angemessen und korrekt kommunizieren kannst. Die Themen sind allgemein gehalten, z. B. Hobbys, Freundschaft, Jobs, Medien, Sport, englischsprachige Länder etc.

Alle Textsorten, denen du in der Prüfung begegnest, sind dir aus deinem Englischunterricht vertraut (Interview, Reportage, Zeitungsartikel, Schilder, Broschüren etc.). In den Prüfungsteilen B, C und D darfst du ein zweisprachiges Wörterbuch benutzen, Smartphones sind aber nicht erlaubt. Rechtschreibfehler führen zu Punktabzug.

Wie arbeitest du mit diesem Heft?

In diesem Heft lernst du durch gezielte Übungen, wie du die Aufgaben zu allen Teilen der Prüfung bearbeiten kannst. Darüber hinaus bekommst du konkrete Prüfungsbeispiele. Das Heft ist deshalb wie folgt aufgebaut:

Das **erste Kapitel**, die *Training Section*, gliedert sich in die fünf Kompetenzbereiche der Prüfung: Hörverstehen, Leseverstehen, Wortschatz und Grammatik, Schreiben sowie Sprechen.

Die *Training Section* enthält:
- Hinweise zum Ablauf und zur Bewertung jedes einzelnen Kompetenzbereichs
- Beispiele und Tipps für die häufigsten Aufgabenformate, die dir in der Prüfung begegnen, also *Multiple choice*, *Matching* etc.
- Strategien zum Umgang mit typischen Schwierigkeiten, wie z. B. Verständnisproblemen

> **Tipp**
>
> Blau umrandete Felder markieren Tipps, die dir bei den Aufgaben helfen.

Es empfiehlt sich, die *Training Section* als erstes durchzuarbeiten, und zwar Kompetenzbereich für Kompetenzbereich. So verschaffst du dir einen Überblick darüber, was du schon gut kannst, wo du noch üben solltest und welche Strategien dir dabei helfen.

Das **zweite Kapitel** bietet dir zwei komplette **Musterprüfungen.** Du lernst dadurch Schritt für Schritt die gesamte Prüfungssituation und den Aufbau der Prüfung kennen.

Wenn du feststellst, dass du mit einem Kompetenzbereich oder einem Aufgabenformat noch Schwierigkeiten hast, gehe zurück in die *Training Section* und wiederhole gezielt die entsprechenden Übungen und Strategien oder nutze die Online-Übungen zu Grammatik und Wortschatz auf www.scook.de.

Die **Tonaufnahmen und Hörtexte** für die *Training Section* und die Musterprüfungen findest du ebenfalls online unter www.scook.de. Das Kopfhörer-Symbol mit Track-Nummer im Heft zeigt dir an, welchen Hörtext du für die Aufgabe anhören musst.

Anhand der **Lösungen** in der Mitte des Heftes kannst du deine Ergebnisse überprüfen und, wenn nötig, verbessern.

Nützliche **Tipps zur Prüfungsvorbereitung** erhältst du auf Seite 76.

Nun kannst du zuversichtlich sein, dass du weißt, was in der Abschlussprüfung an der Hauptschule in Baden-Württemberg auf dich zukommt, und dass du die unterschiedlichen Aufgabenstellungen geübt hast und kennst.

> Zusätzlich kannst du dein Grundwissen in den Bereichen Grammatik und Wortschatz mithilfe von Online-Übungen wiederholen und vertiefen. Nutze dazu den Zugangscode auf Seite 1 (www.scook.de).
>
> Ebenfalls online findest du die Tonaufnahmen zu den Höraufgaben als MP3-Downloads und die dazugehörigen Hörtexte. Nutze dazu ebenfalls den Code von Seite 1.

Viel Spaß beim Training mit diesem Heft und viel Erfolg bei der Prüfung!

Teil A: *Listening comprehension* (Hörverstehen)

1. Ablauf und Bewertung

Der Ablauf beim Hörverstehen

Für den Prüfungsteil Hörverstehen (Teil A der Prüfung) hast du 30 Minuten Zeit.

Das Hörverstehen besteht aus vier gleichwertigen Teilen bzw. Aufgaben (Parts 1–4), die thematisch nicht miteinander zusammenhängen. In jedem dieser Parts hörst du einen oder mehrere Hörtexte in unterschiedlichen Längen. Dazu löst du dann verschiedene Aufgaben, z. B.:
- Fragen mithilfe von drei vorgegebenen Antwortmöglichkeiten beantworten *(Multiple choice)*
- vorgegebene Satzanfänge mithilfe von drei möglichen Satzenden vervollständigen *(Multiple choice)*
- Informationen stichwortartig in einer vorgegebenen Tabelle ergänzen *(Fill in the table)*
- Zuordnungsaufgaben bearbeiten *(Matching)*

Zunächst hast du einige Minuten Zeit, um die Aufgaben durchzulesen. Dann wird die Tonaufnahme mit den vier Parts ohne Unterbrechung abgespielt (ca. 20–25 Minuten). Sie enthält noch einmal die Aufgabenstellungen sowie die eigentlichen Hörtexte, die du jeweils zweimal hintereinander hörst. Anschließend wird dir gesagt, wie viele Minuten du Zeit hast, um deine Lösungen aufzuschreiben.

Am Ende von Teil A der Prüfung werden die Blätter eingesammelt und du hast 15 Minuten Pause.

Die Bewertung der Aufgaben zum Hörverstehen

Beim Hörverstehen kannst du insgesamt 20 Punkte erreichen. Das Hörverstehen macht also 25 % deiner schriftlichen Prüfungsnote aus. Deine Antwort wird entweder als richtig oder als falsch bewertet. Kreuzt du mehr Lösungen an als gefordert, so verlierst du Punkte. Halbe Punkte erhältst du, wenn z. B. zwei Wörter in ein Tabellenfeld eingetragen werden müssen, du aber nur eins hinschreibst oder richtig hast.

Ein Wörterbuch ist beim Hörverstehen nicht erlaubt. Du brauchst aber keine Angst vor Rechtschreibfehlern in deinen Antworten zu haben. Solange man versteht, was du geschrieben hast, werden dir in diesem Prüfungsteil keine Punkte abgezogen.

2. Aufgabenformate in Baden-Württemberg

In diesem Kapitel lernst du beispielhaft die wichtigsten Aufgabenformate kennen, die dir beim Hauptschulabschluss in Baden-Württemberg im Bereich Hörverstehen begegnen können.

Die Tipp-Kästen enthalten nützliche Strategien, wie du mit häufigen Schwierigkeiten umgehen kannst.

Auswahlaufgaben mit Fragen *(Multiple choice)*

Bei diesem Aufgabentyp hörst du meist fünf kurze Dialoge. Zu jedem Dialog beantwortest du eine Frage und erhältst dafür drei Antwortmöglichkeiten.

Hier in der *Training Section* ist die Aufgabe gekürzt: Du hörst **drei** kurze Dialoge und bearbeitest dazu jeweils eine Multiple-choice-Frage. Aufgaben in voller Länge findest du bei den Musterprüfungen ab Seite 57.

Short conversations

You will hear three short conversations.
There is one question for each conversation.

Mark A, B or C.

a) Where will Olivia and her friends probably go?

    A ☐ ice-skating

    B ☐ shopping

    C ☐ to a museum

b) When should Mrs Taylor be at the dentist?

    A ☐ Tuesday, late morning

    B ☐ Wednesday morning

    C ☐ Thursday, early afternoon

c) What has the woman lost?

    A ☐ her money

    B ☐ her keys

    C ☐ her phone

> **Tipp**
>
> Die Hörtexte sind kurz, enthalten aber viele Details. Um zu wissen, worauf du beim Hören achten musst, solltest du die Aufgaben vorher einmal durchlesen! So kannst du deine Aufmerksamkeit besser auf die Details lenken, die für die Aufgabe wichtig sind.

Auswahlaufgaben mit Satzanfängen (Multiple choice)

Bei diesem Aufgabentyp hörst du meistens einen etwas längeren Dialog. Du erhältst fünf Satzanfänge, die du mithilfe von drei vorgegebenen Satzenden vervollständigen sollst.

You will hear a conversation between two friends about a visit to Krakow in Poland.

Mark A, B or C.

A visit to Krakow

a) Tim travelled to Krakow …

    A ☐ by train.

    B ☐ by plane.

    C ☐ by car.

> **Tipp**
>
> Bei Multiple-choice-Aufgaben hörst du oft nicht genau das gleiche Wort wie in den Lösungsmöglichkeiten A, B oder C, sondern andere Formulierungen, z. B. in a):
>
> • Statt *by train* hörst du vielleicht *at the station*.
> • Statt *car* hörst du vielleicht *we drove*.
>
> Welche Formulierung könnte statt *by plane* kommen?

b) In Krakow Tim stayed …

A ☐ with a family member.

B ☐ with a friend in the town centre.

C ☐ in town, but not in the centre.

Tipp

Es kann sein, dass du ein Wort im Hörtext nicht kennst – wie hier wahrscheinlich *suburb*. Trotzdem kannst du oft auf die richtige Lösung kommen, wenn du das **Ausschlussverfahren** anwendest, z. B. in b):
Du wirst hören, dass Tim seine Unterkunft im Internet bucht. Dadurch fallen bereits zwei Lösungsmöglichkeiten weg!

c) In Krakow Tim visited …

A ☐ places with few tourists.

B ☐ the main tourist sights.

C ☐ places with not too many people.

Tipp

Vorsicht bei identischen Wörtern in Hörtext und Aufgabe! Sie deuten nicht unbedingt auf die richtige Lösung hin, z. B. in c):
Im Hörtext kommt *main tourist sites* vor – wie in Lösung **B**. Ist **B** folglich die richtige Lösung? Nein! Denn im Hörtext heißt es __ __ __ *the main tourist sites!*

d) Tim made himself understood with English and …

A ☐ no Polish, but lots of smiles.

B ☐ a little Polish and making signs.

C ☐ Polish that he learned at school.

Tipp

Bei Multiple-choice-Aufgaben werden einzelne Wörter aus dem Hörtext oft ersetzt durch:
• **Synonyme** (Wörter und Ausdrücke mit ähnlicher Bedeutung, wie *great – wonderful*)
• **Antonyme** (Wörter und Ausdrücke mit gegensätzlicher Bedeutung, wie *great – awful / not great at all*)

Dieses Wissen kann dir helfen, die richtige Lösung zu finden, z. B. in d):

Synonyme:
a few words of Polish im Hörtext = *a little Polish* in **B**
use your hands im Hörtext   = _____ in **B**

Also ist **B** wahrscheinlich die richtige Antwort.

Antonyme:
taught myself im Hörtext   ≠ *learned at school* in **C**
a few words of Polish im Hörtext ≠ _____ in **A**

Also scheiden **A** und **C** wahrscheinlich aus.

e) Tim thinks that …

A ☐ Krakow is too expensive.

B ☐ every visitor should know a few words of Polish.

C ☐ Krakow is changing fast.

Notizen in einer Tabelle anfertigen *(Fill in the table)*

Bei diesem Aufgabentyp musst du gezielt bestimmte Informationen aus dem Hörtext heraushören und notieren. Dies tust du, indem du vorgegebene Notizen stichwortartig ergänzt, meist in einer Tabelle.

A tourist attraction in Brighton

You will hear a reporter who is talking about a new tourist attraction in Brighton.

Listen and complete the table.

Tipp

Achte beim Zuhören auf Schlüsselwörter *(key words)*, die zu den Vorgaben in der Tabelle passen.
Die Informationen sind im Hörtext meist in der gleichen Reihenfolge wie in der Tabelle angeordnet.
Du kannst die Informationen also der Reihe nach notieren.

The British Airways i360 – a tourist attraction in Brighton		
	location of the reporter	*seafront*
a)	was opened in (month, year)	
b)	number of visitors to Brighton every year:	
c)	from the top you can enjoy …	
d)	architects designed another famous attraction in …	
e)	price for a ride for tourists:	£

Tipp

Bei diesem Aufgabentyp geht es – neben Namen und Orten – oft um Zahlen.
Wiederhole daher vor der Prüfung die Kardinalzahlen *(one, two, three …)*, Ordinalzahlen *(first, second, third …)*,
Jahreszahlen (1680, 1860 …), Jahrhunderte (1900–1999: *20th century*) etc.!

Zuordnungsaufgaben *(Matching)*

Bei diesem Aufgabentyp hörst du in der Regel einen etwas längeren Dialog. Anschließend sollst du fünf Begriffen aus dem Hörtext (Personen, Themen, Orten, …) jeweils eine von meist acht vorgegebenen Lösungsmöglichkeiten zuordnen.

Skyways in the US and Canada

You will hear part of an interview with an architect about 'skyways' in Canada and the US. What does 'skyway' mean in each place?

Write a letter, A–H, next to each place.

Skyway in Calgary

a)	Calgary	☐	A drive-in cinema
b)	Burlington	☐	B tram in a city
c)	Stoney Creek	☐	C paragliding centre
d)	Kissimmee	☐	D bridge
e)	Jacksonville	☐	E cafe with a view
			F walkway above street level
			G airline
			H platform

Tipp

Meistens sind mehr Lösungsmöglichkeiten als Begriffe vorgegeben. In diesem Beispiel bleiben drei Lösungen übrig. Wenn du beim ersten Hören nicht alle Begriffe zuordnen kannst, nutze auch das zweite Hören.

3. Umgang mit Verständnisproblemen

Die Hörtexte in der Abschlussprüfung enthalten manchmal Wörter, die du vielleicht nicht kennst oder die du nicht verstehst, weil sie von anderen Geräuschen im Prüfungsraum überdeckt werden. Das ist ganz normal. Also keine Panik – es gibt Strategien, die dir helfen, die wesentlichen Inhalte trotzdem zu erfassen und die Aufgabe zu lösen. In diesem Kapitel werden anhand der Tonspur eines Werbefilms über die Niagarafälle die wichtigsten Strategien vorgestellt. Diese Strategien kannst du auch für die Aufgaben zum Leseverstehen nutzen.

> **Tipp**
>
> Die Tonaufnahmen in diesem Kapitel enthalten Störgeräusche, die einige Textstellen unverständlich machen (∩ 5, ∩ 7, ∩ 9). Um dir zu verdeutlichen, dass du viele Aufgaben trotzdem lösen kannst, werden in diesem Kapitel die Hörtexte mit abgedruckt und die unverständlichen Stellen geschwärzt. Bei anderen Aufgaben kannst du mithilfe der Tipps zumindest Vermutungen anstellen.
> Wenn du die Aufgaben gelöst hast, hörst du die Tonaufnahme jeweils ein zweites Mal ohne Störgeräusche (∩ 6, ∩ 8, ∩ 10). Nun kannst du überprüfen, ob deine Antworten und Vermutungen richtig waren.

Auswahlaufgaben mit Satzanfängen *(Multiple choice)*

The Niagara Falls (Part 1)

> 1. You will hear the audio track of a film about the Niagara Falls.
>
> Mark A, B or C.
> You can read the text on page 11.

a) The Horseshoe Falls are …

- **A** ☐ in Buffalo.
- **B** ☐ only in Canada.
- **C** ☐ in Canada and the USA.

> **Tipp**
>
> Wenn du bei a) nicht gleich auf die richtige Antwort kommst, wende das **Ausschlussverfahren** an:
> • Welche Stelle im Hörtext schließt Antwort A aus?
> • Zwischen B und C kannst du dich noch nicht entscheiden: Im Hörtext könnte es nämlich heißen *only* in Canada, *mainly* in Canada, *partly* in Canada oder *fully* in Canada.
>
> Also wirst du beim zweiten Hören an dieser Stelle besonders gut hinhören müssen. Aber jetzt kannst du gezielt zwischen zwei möglichen Antworten entscheiden – das ist leichter als zwischen dreien.

b) The people on the boat wear …

- **A** ☐ raincoats.
- **B** ☐ safety gloves.
- **C** ☐ special glasses.

> **Tipp**
>
> Bei b) kannst du dir helfen, indem du Vermutungen anstellst. Wovor müssen sich die Touristen schützen? Gefahren für Hände oder Augen werden im Hörtext nicht erwähnt. Dafür erfährst du aber, dass die Touristen nass werden. Wie können sie sich davor schützen?

Welcome to the Niagara Falls! These astonishing natural waterfalls are on the border between the USA and Canada. They consist of three waterfalls. The two smaller ones are in the USA. But these amazing falls, called the Horseshoe Falls, are the biggest and they're ▮▮▮ in Canada. The Niagara Falls are located near important urban centres. It only takes half an hour by car to get to Buffalo.

These tourists have just landed at Buffalo International Airport and they're on their way to see the famous falls. In fact, about 30 million people visit the Niagara Falls each year!

And this group is going on the very popular *Maid of the Mist* tour – a boat tour to the bottom of the waterfalls. The air here is full of spray from the splashing water. That's why everyone here is wearing ▮▮▮▮▮. But don't be fooled – most of them are going to get wet anyway. Oh. Here comes the next shower!

6

2. Now listen to part one of the audio track again. This time it's complete. Note the exact words in the recording.

Then check your answers in task 1.

a) ... the Horseshoe Falls are the biggest and they're _____ in Canada.

b) ... that's why everyone here is wearing _____.

Auswahlaufgaben mit Fragen *(Multiple choice)*

The Niagara Falls (Part 2)

7

1. You will hear more about the Niagara Falls.

Mark A, B or C.
You can read the text on page 12.

a) Why were the falls on the American side made into a state park?

A ☐ because Central Park is a state park too

B ☐ to make tourists pay to get in

C ☐ to protect the environment

b) Where do the tourists stand?

A ☐ below the falls

B ☐ above the falls

C ☐ behind the falls

Tipp

Keine Panik, wenn du nicht alle Details über den Nationalpark *(state park)* verstanden hast! Bei **a)** helfen dir folgende Strategien:
- Nutze dein **Weltwissen**! Welchen Zweck haben Nationalparks normalerweise? Die Antwort hierauf spricht für Lösung __.
- **Ausschlussverfahren**: Was erfährst du über den Eintritt? Die Antwort hierauf schließt Lösung __ aus.
- Achte nun beim **zweiten Hören** auf die **Schlüsselwörter** aus deiner vermuteten Lösung.

Tipp

In den Lösungsmöglichkeiten werden oft Synonyme für Wörter aus dem Hörtext verwendet. Im Hörtext lautet die Ortsangabe *right next to the top*. Welche Lösung bedeutet ungefähr das gleiche?

Accessing the falls is easy. That's great because it means that thousands of people can come and see the fantastic sight. But it also means that the falls have to be well protected ████████████. In fact, these falls on the American side are actually part of the country's oldest state park. It was designed by the same man who laid out this well-known park. Do you recognize it? It's Central Park in New York City. Luckily state parks don't charge entrance – so you don't have to pay to see the falls. Tourists can stand right next to the top of the Horseshoe Falls and watch the water spilling over. Isn't it amazing?

5

10

 8

2. Now listen to part two of the audio track again. This time it's complete. Note the exact words in the recording.

Then check your answers in task 1.

... the falls have to be well protected _____.

Notizen in einer Tabelle anfertigen *(Fill in the table)*

The Niagara Falls (Part 3)

 9

1. You will hear part 3 of the audio track about the Niagara Falls. Listen and complete the table. You can read the text on page 13.

The Niagara Falls – Annie Taylor	
a)	year of first ride over the falls:	
b)	Annie Taylor's age:	
c)	reason for the first ride:	needed
d)	result of the first ride:	Her _____ was hurt.

Tipp

Selbst wenn du die Textstelle nicht verstanden hast, in der gesagt wird, warum sich Annie Taylor den Wasserfall hinunterstürzte, kannst du Aufgabe c) trotzdem lösen. Was erfährst du nämlich über ihren Ehemann und ihren Sohn? Sie waren gestorben. Und was folgte daraus für eine Frau in der damaligen Zeit? Sie brauchte _____.

Auch für d) musst du nicht alle Details über ihre Verletzungen verstehen. Hier wird nur das verletzte Körperteil verlangt. Aber Achtung! Es werden auch unverletzte Körperteile erwähnt!

Sometimes people have gone over the falls. Some have even done it by choice.

This is Annie Taylor. She was the first person to ride over the Niagara Falls, way back in 1901, on her 63rd birthday. After her husband and son had died, Annie was facing poverty and decided to go over the falls to ▮▮▮▮▮▮▮. And guess what she used to cross the falls – this thing. That's right: a wooden barrel. The sort of barrel that was used to store wine or beer. Crazy, isn't it? She put cushions and a mattress inside, and asked some friends to push the barrel in the right direction at the top – and other friends to open it when she got to the bottom of the falls. And she did. She went over the top of the falls, the barrel fell, and when her friends opened it, she was alive. But although Annie (amazingly!) came out with no broken bones, she did hurt her head: it ▮▮▮▮▮.

After her crazy experiment, Annie warned other people against doing the same thing. We'll take your advice, Annie.

2. Now listen to part three of the audio track again. This time it's complete. Note the exact words in the recording.

Then check your answers in task 1.

a) Annie (...) decided to go over the falls to _____ .

b) But although Annie (amazingly!) came out with no broken bones, she did hurt her head:

it _____ .

4. Hörverstehen – *Now you*

Nun kannst du einige Aufgabenformate und Strategien, die du auf den letzten Seiten kennen gelernt hast, bei ausgewählten Aufgaben zum Hörverstehen gezielt üben. Grundlage dafür sind ein Dialog über ein Radrennen in England sowie ein Radio-Interview über die jamaikanische Reggae-Legende Bob Marley. Zu Übungszwecken sind diese Hörtexte etwas länger als in der Prüfung.

Auswahlaufgaben mit Satzanfängen und Fragen *(Multiple choice)*

Two fantastic cycle races

You will hear a conversation between two friends about a cycling race in England.

Mark A, B or C.

Yellow bicycle on the city walls of York, 2014

a) Where did the 2014 *Tour de France* begin?

A ☐ in France

B ☐ in Bradford

C ☐ in Yorkshire

b) During the race in Yorkshire, cycling fans …

    A ☐ rode yellow bicycles.

    B ☐ bought yellow bicycles.

    C ☐ painted old bicycles yellow.

c) The organizers of the *Tour de France* …

    A ☐ planned for large crowds.

    B ☐ didn't expect so many fans.

    C ☐ were sad about the small number of fans.

d) What did people in Yorkshire want after the 2014 race?

    A ☐ their own cycling race

    B ☐ a bigger race

    C ☐ new roads

e) Why is the *Tour de Yorkshire* so difficult?

    A ☐ It's very long.

    B ☐ There are many hills.

    C ☐ The roads are too wide.

Notizen in einer Tabelle anfertigen *(Fill in the table)*

Bob Marley

12

You will hear a radio interview with Reggae expert Gwen Devlin about the Jamaican singer Bob Marley.

Listen and complete the table.

Bob Marley – the most famous Jamaican ever?			
	a)	born in (country, year)	in in
	b)	father was from …	
	c)	lived in Trenchtown with his …	
	d)	name of his first band:	
	e)	name of a famous song:	

Teil B: *Text-based tasks* (Leseverstehen)

1. Ablauf und Bewertung

Für die Prüfungsteile B *(Text-based tasks)*, C *(Use of language)* und D *(Writing)* hast du 90 Minuten Zeit, die du dir frei einteilen kannst. Plane also genügend Zeit für jeden Prüfungsteil ein und bedenke, dass du am Ende auch noch Zeit zum Korrekturlesen benötigst.

Du kannst selbst entscheiden, mit welchem Prüfungsteil du anfängst. Es ist aber hilfreich, mit Teil B zu beginnen. So lernst du das Thema sowie Wortschatz und Wendungen kennen, die du unter Umständen auch in den Teilen C und D verwenden kannst.

Das Leseverstehen besteht aus fünf Teilen bzw. Aufgaben (Parts 1–5), z. B.:
- verschiedene kürzere Texte wie Hinweisschilder *(signs)* lesen und aus drei Möglichkeiten die passende Erklärung auswählen *(Multiple choice)*
- einen längeren Text lesen und dazu verschiedene Aufgaben lösen:
  - Textabschnitten eine passende Überschrift zuordnen *(Matching)*
  - vorgegebene Satzanfänge mithilfe von drei möglichen Satzenden vervollständigen *(Multiple choice)*
  - zu vorgegebenen Formulierungen eine bedeutungsgleiche Entsprechung im Text finden
  - Aussagen überprüfen *(true, false, not in the text)*

Du kannst beim Leseverstehen 25 Punkte erreichen. Damit wird dieser Teil der schriftlichen Prüfung am stärksten gewichtet.

Beim Leseverstehen darfst du ein zweisprachiges Wörterbuch verwenden. Kreuzt du bei Multiple-choice-Aufgaben mehr Lösungen an als gefordert, so verlierst du Punkte.

> **Tipp**
>
> Wichtig! In der Prüfung bekommst du für die Prüfungsteile B, C und D weißes Papier, auf dem du deine Lösungen notieren musst. Lösungen, die du auf dem Aufgabenblatt einträgst, werden nicht bewertet!
>
> Achte darauf, deine Lösungen so zu notieren, dass man sie klar zu den Aufgaben zuordnen kann (Nummerierung, z. B. Teil B, Part 1: …).

2. Aufgabenformate in Baden-Württemberg

In diesem Kapitel lernst du beispielhaft die wichtigsten Aufgabenformate kennen, die dir beim Hauptschulabschluss in Baden-Württemberg im Bereich Leseverstehen begegnen können.

Die Tipp-Kästen enthalten nützliche Strategien, wie du mit häufigen Schwierigkeiten umgehen kannst.

Beachte: Die Lesetexte in der *Training Section* dienen als Beispiele für bestimmte Aufgabenformate. Sie sind daher teilweise deutlich kürzer als in der Abschlussprüfung. Längere Lesetexte findest du in den Musterprüfungen ab Seite 57.

Kürzere Texte: Auswahlaufgaben mit Erklärungen *(Multiple choice)*

Bei diesem Aufgabentyp musst du die Texte (meist Warn- oder Hinweisschilder) genau lesen und dann entscheiden, welche der Aussagen A–C den Inhalt der Schilder am besten wiedergibt.

> **Tipp**
>
> Es geht bei dieser Aufgabe nicht darum, was sein könnte, sondern was konkret mit diesem Schild gemeint ist. Lies daher den Text und die Lösungen A–C gründlich. Nur eine Lösung ist richtig!

Understanding signs

What information do these signs give you? Write down the correct letters (A–C).

a)

BEACH ACCESS
BEHIND RESTROOMS
AND SHOWERS

A The showers are on the beach.

B You can get to the beach behind the showers.

C You can rent beach cabins here.

Tipp

Du musst hier nicht jedes Wort kennen. Es reicht, wenn du die Schlüsselwörter verstehst: *beach, behind* und *showers*.

b)

CAUTION
RATTLESNAKES
COMMON ON ISLAND

A Don't take pictures of snakes on this island.

B You can learn to play the drums on this island.

C There are dangerous animals on this island.

Tipp

Du kennst *caution* und *common* nicht? Nutze die Schlüsselwörter *snake* und *island* und dein Weltwissen!

c)

SHELTER IS AVAILABLE
ON A FIRST COME
FIRST SERVED BASIS

A You can use the shelter if it has space.

B You have to make a reservation for the shelter.

C They serve food and drink at the shelter.

d)

DANGER! ALLIGATORS!
DO NOT FEED OR
MOLEST. FEEDING THEM
CAN RESULT IN THEM
MISTAKING A HAND FOR
A HANDOUT.

A The alligators could get used to being fed.

B The alligators might see you as a danger and get aggressive.

C The alligators might think your hand is food.

e)

RESTRICTED WILDLIFE
AREA. FOR NEXT 5 MILES
PHOTOGRAPHY AND
OBSERVATION OF
WILDLIFE PERMITTED
FROM ROAD ONLY.

A You mustn't leave the road if you want to take pictures.

B You are not allowed to take pictures on the road.

C You can take pictures of wild animals everywhere in this area.

Längerer Text: verschiedene Formate

Die nächsten Aufgaben basieren in der Regel auf demselben Lesetext, der ca. eine Seite lang ist. Zu diesem Lesetext bearbeitest du dann verschiedene Aufgabenformate, die nun vorgestellt werden. Hier in der *Training Section* gibt es zu Übungszwecken zwei etwas kürzere Texte für je zwei Aufgabenformate. Längere Texte findest du in den Musterprüfungen ab Seite 57.

Überschriften zuordnen *(Matching)*

Bei diesem Aufgabenformat erhältst du meist fünf (hier: vier) Überschriften, die du einer gleichen Anzahl an Textabschnitten zuordnen sollst. Fang mit den Zuordnungen an, die dir am leichtesten fallen.

> Read the text about Aboriginal people in Australia. Match the letter of the headings with the correct number of the parts of the text.
>
> Write down the correct answers. Example: 5) – e)

1)	lines 1–5	**a)**	A different life	_____
2)	lines 6–8	**b)**	A terrible law	_____
3)	lines 9–13	**c)**	Large numbers	_____
4)	lines 14–18	**d)**	All alone	_____

Tipp

Was hilft dir hier?

- **Synonyme** (Wörter mit ähnlicher Bedeutung), z. B.:
  law (in der Aufgabe) = *rule* (im Text)
  alone (in der Aufgabe) = ___ ___ ___ ___ ___ ___
  (im Text)

- **Sammelbegriffe**, die stellvertretend für Beispiele im Text stehen, z. B.:
  large numbers (in der Aufgabe) = 250,000/500,000 (im Text)

Australia's Stolen Generations – a text from a museum

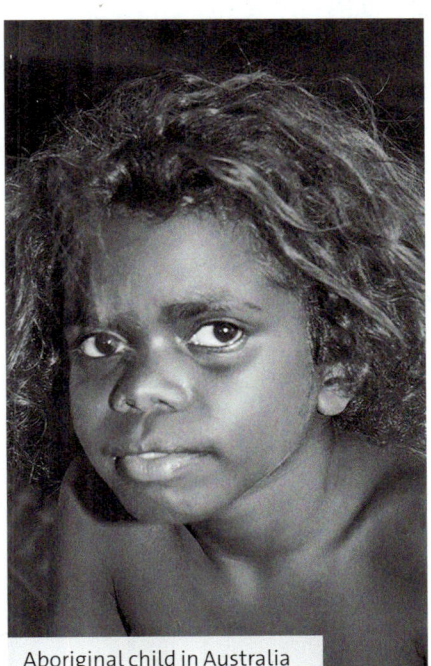

In 1915 the government of New South Wales in Australia made a new rule that allowed officials to take Aboriginal children away from their mothers and fathers – even against their will. Other Australian states later did
5 the same.

This was the fate of over 250,000 Aboriginal children, some say as many as 500,000, who had to leave their homes.

The children from Aboriginal families were housed
10 in new English-speaking homes where they were not allowed to speak their own language. And they were given the typical foods of white Australians, even though they weren't used to it.

The parents were not told where their children were,
15 and the children were not allowed to get in touch with their parents. The result was that the children had no contact with their families, their language, their music and their former way of life.

Aboriginal child in Australia

Richtig-/Falsch-Aufgaben *(True, false or not in the text?)*

Bei diesem Aufgabentyp erhältst du in der Regel fünf (hier: vier) Aussagen zum Inhalt des Textes. Oft wird die Information aus dem Text etwas umformuliert und du musst entscheiden, ob die Aussage in Bezug auf den Text noch korrekt ist oder falsch oder ob sie gar nicht im Text enthalten ist.

> Read the text about Aboriginal people in Australia again. Decide whether the statements are 'true', 'false' or 'not in the text'.
>
> Write down the correct answers. Example: f) – not in the text

a) The law that allowed Aboriginal children to be taken away was introduced in the early 20th century.

_____

b) More than half a million Aboriginal children were taken away from their families.

_____

c) Luckily some nicer officers allowed the parents to look for their children.

_____

d) After a few years the Aboriginal children lost touch with their culture.

_____

Tipp

Auch Zahlen können auf verschiedene Weise ausgedrückt werden. Überprüfe in a) und b):

im Text:	in der Aufgabe:	Ist die Bedeutung gleich oder ähnlich?
in 1915	in the early 20th century	ja / nein
250,000 to 500,000	more than half a million	ja / nein

Bedeutung gleich oder ähnlich: Aussage ist wahrscheinlich richtig!
Bedeutung unterscheidet sich stark: Aussage ist wahrscheinlich falsch!

Tipp

Weitere Möglichkeiten, die gleiche Information etwas anders zu formulieren, z. B. in d):

ein Sammelbegriff statt einzelner Begriffe:

im Text:	in der Aufgabe:
families, language, music, way of life	_ _ _ _ _ _ _

synonyme Formulierungen:

im Text:	in der Aufgabe:
had no contact with ...	They lost _ _ _ _ _ with ...

Auswahlaufgaben mit Satzanfängen *(Multiple choice)*

Eine weitere typische Aufgabe ist das Vervollständigen von Satzanfängen mithilfe einer Auswahl an Möglichkeiten. In der Regel werden fünf (hier: vier) Satzanfänge mit je drei Lösungsmöglichkeiten vorgegeben.

> Read the beginning of the short story *Kasun*. Complete the sentences by choosing the correct ending according to the text.
>
> Write down the correct answers. Example: 5) – A)

Kasun's first day at a new school

On the first day at my new school in Colombo I was scared stiff. Not that I showed it, of course. I pretended to be relaxed while all the time my knees were like jelly.

5 My mum appeared to be calm, but I knew her better than that. Her red eyes told their own story.

When I got to school, all the other kids in Grade 9 seemed to know each other, maybe 10 because they all lived in Colombo. Even the teachers had the same accent as they did. But I was from Kuruwita, a smaller town outside the capital, and I felt like a fish out of water.

"Hey, what's your name?"
I turned round and saw a big boy. He was 15 smiling. But was he talking to me? Or to somebody behind me? I didn't dare answer.

"Hey, what's the problem?" said the boy and took a step closer to me. I couldn't help see his big hands. Was he going to hit me? 20

"Do you think I'm going to bite you? Hi. I'm Sahan."

"I ... I'm Kasun," I stuttered. "I'm not from Colombo. I'm from Kuruwita, but I ..."

"Hey, calm down, you're talking too fast," 25 laughed Sahan.

1) On his first day of school Kasun felt ...

A ☐ excited.

B ☐ out of place.

C ☐ relaxed.

> **Tipp**
>
> Finde die richtige Stelle im Text. Wo geht es um Kasuns Gefühle? Er vergleicht sich hier mit einem Fisch auf dem Trockenen: Wie fühlt sich wohl ein solcher Fisch?

2) The other kids in Kasun's class ...

A ☐ probably all came from the same city.

B ☐ were from Kuruwita, too.

C ☐ seemed to know Kasun's mother.

> **Tipp**
>
> Wenn du dir unsicher bist, nutze das Ausschlussverfahren:
>
> Welcher Satz im Text schließt Lösung **B** aus?
>
> Nun bleiben noch zwei mögliche Lösungen. Welche ist im Zusammenhang des Textes wahrscheinlicher?

3) The teachers ...

A ☐ didn't speak to Kasun.

B ☐ spoke a different language.

C ☐ spoke like most of the students.

> **Tipp**
>
> Such die Textstelle, wo es um Kasuns Lehrer geht. Dort findet sich ein Wort, das du vielleicht nicht kennst *(accent)*. Aber es gibt ein sehr ähnliches Wort im Deutschen! Wenn du dir immer noch unsicher bist, verwende dein Wörterbuch!

4) The big boy ...

A ☐ wanted to fight with Kasun.

B ☐ tried to be friendly.

C ☐ wasn't talking to Kasun at all.

Synonyme Textstellen *(Sentence parts that mean the same)*

Bei diesem Aufgabenformat erhältst du fünf (hier: vier) Sätze oder Teile von Sätzen. Es handelt sich um andere Formulierungen für Sätze aus dem Text. Deine Aufgabe besteht darin, im Text die Sätze zu finden, die im Wesentlichen das gleiche bedeuten wie die Sätze aus der Aufgabe.

> Read the text from *Kasun* again. Find the corresponding sentence parts or sentences in the text that mean the same and write them down.

a) I was so frightened that I could hardly move.

_____

_____

Tipp

Auch bei diesem Aufgabenformat kommen häufig Synonyme zum Einsatz. Welche Synonyme kennst du für *frightened* in a)? Such dann die entsprechende Textstelle.

b) I felt so nervous that I was unstable on my legs.

_____

_____

c) It was obvious that she had cried.

_____

_____

Tipp

Selbst, wenn du *obvious* in c) nicht kennst, kannst du diese Aufgabe lösen:
- Es gibt nur eine *she* im Text, nämlich _____ . Suche also an der Stelle im Text, wo es um diese Person geht.
- Was passiert, wenn man weint? Suche die Stelle im Text, die das beschreibt.

d) I had a strong feeling that I didn't belong here.

_____

_____

Tipp

Wenn du glaubst, dass du die richtige Stelle im Text gefunden hast, setze die Formulierung aus der Aufgabe an diese Stelle und kontrolliere, ob der Text dann noch dasselbe aussagt. Ziehe dafür auch den Satz davor und den Satz danach heran.

Achtung! Sei beim Abschreiben der von dir gefundenen Textstelle besonders gründlich. Fehler beim Abschreiben führen zum Verlust von Punkten!

3. Umgang mit Verständnisproblemen

Die Lesetexte in der Prüfung enthalten manchmal Wörter, die du nicht kennst. Zwar kannst du sie in deinem Wörterbuch nachschlagen, aber das ist manchmal zeitaufwändig. Mit einigen Strategien kannst du die Aufgaben oft auch lösen, ohne den Umweg über dein Wörterbuch zu gehen. Wenn du auf ein unbekanntes Wort triffst, kannst du es zunächst markieren und versuchen, es dir zu erschließen, z. B. aus dem Zusammenhang oder durch ähnliche Wörter, die du kennst. Bei einigen Aufgaben genügt es auch, wenn du die allgemeine Aussage des Textes verstehst, selbst wenn du nicht jedes Wort kennst. Dieses Kapitel zeigt dir einige wichtige Strategien anhand einer Broschüre über die Everglades.

The Everglades

Die Everglades sind ein tropisches Naturschutzgebiet in Florida. Dieser Text stammt aus einer Informationsbroschüre, in der auf Straßenarbeiten in dem Gebiet aufmerksam gemacht wird.

> Neu – kannst du den Sinn aus bekannten Wörtern erschließen? Vielleicht ist es aber für deine Antwort auch unwichtig!

> Vielleicht neu – aber du kannst die Bedeutung aus dem Zusammenhang erschließen: Es geht um den Lebensraum der Alligatoren.

> Neu – aber aus dem Zusammenhang kannst du schließen: Die Haustiere sind in den Everglades, weil die Menschen sie herausgelassen haben.

> Neu – aber du kennst *danger* = Gefahr.

> Du kennst *wet* und *land*. Was könnten also *wetlands* sein?

> Neues Verb – aber du kennst *dry* = trocken.

> Neu – aber aus dem Zusammenhang kannst du schließen: Dieser Erdwall hindert das Wasser am Fließen.

1 The wetlands of the Everglades in the south of the state of Florida are famous for their alligators, snakes, turtles and other wildlife, which tourists can sometimes catch sight of from airboats or on
5   specially-provided hiking trails. Visitor centers show alligators feeding and inform tourists about how the alligators' environment is endangered.

2 In fact, the Everglades are facing huge environmental issues. Its lakes and rivers are polluted by
10   dirty waste water from the city of Miami. And pets released into the Everglades by inhabitants of the city have become a danger to the original wildlife.

3 But the biggest headache of all is that the wetlands are drying out. This is partly because, in the
15   1960s, the slow-flowing Kissimmee River was replaced by a dead straight canal that makes the water flow away too quickly. And what makes it worse is that the U.S. Highway 41, which was completed in 1928, cuts through 275 miles of the Everglades from
20   east to west on a wall of earth. This prevents water from flowing into the southern part of the Everglades.

4 It has now been decided that parts of the canal will be filled in to allow the water to flow into the slower river. And a mile-long stretch of Highway 41 will be
25   made into a bridge to allow water to pass under it.

Überschriften zuordnen *(Matching)*

> Read the brochure about the Everglades. Match the letter of the headings with the correct number of the parts of the text. Write down the correct answers. Example: 5) – e)

1) lines 1–7   **a)** Pollution problems   _____

2) lines 8–12   **b)** Educating the public   _____

3) lines 13–21   **c)** What can be done?   _____

4) lines 22–25   **d)** Mistakes of the past   _____

Tipp

Wie kannst du eine Überschrift zuordnen, wenn du nicht alle Wörter kennst? Beispiel: In Überschrift a) kennst du *pollution* vielleicht nicht. Keine Panik:
1. Nur in zwei Abschnitten geht es um Probleme, nämlich ____ und ____. Das grenzt die Auswahl ein.
2. Zu einem dieser beiden Abschnitte passt auch eine andere Überschrift. Es geht darin um Probleme der Vergangenheit. Dieser Abschnitt fällt also auch raus: ____

Also gehört Überschrift a) wahrscheinlich zu Abschnitt ____ und damit zu Lösung ____.

Richtig-/Falsch-Aufgaben *(True, false or not in the text?)*

> Decide whether the statements are 'true', 'false' or 'not in the text'. Write down the correct answers. Example: f) – false

a) Luckily the environment in which the alligators live is not really in danger.   _____

b) People from Miami sometimes try to catch wild animals in the Everglades.   _____

c) The wetlands of the Everglades aren't getting enough water.   _____

d) A highway was built through the Everglades in the 19th century.   _____

e) The plan now is to build a bridge over the Highway, so that the water can flow.   _____

Tipp

Sätze a) + c): Was ist, wenn du die entscheidenden Textstellen nicht verstanden hast, weil du einige Wörter nicht kennst? Denke an Wortfamilien:

Familie *danger*: *danger* (Nomen), *dangerous* (Adjektiv), *to endanger* (Verb), …

Familie *wet*: *wet* (Adjektiv), *to wet* (Verb), *wetness* (Nomen), *wetlands* (Nomen), …

Familie *dry*: *dry* (Adjektiv), *hairdryer* (Nomen), *to dry (out)* (Verb), …

So kannst du dir den Sinn der entscheidenden Sätze erschließen und die Aufgabe lösen. Natürlich hilft dir hier auch der Zusammenhang weiter.

Tipp

Satz b): Die entscheidende Stelle ist Absatz **2**, aber du kennst *release* nicht? Versuche, dir den Sinn des Satzes auch ohne *release* zu erschließen:

… pets … have become a danger to the original wildlife.

Die Haustiere der Bewohner von Miami bringen also Wildtiere in Gefahr. Es ist aber keine Rede davon, dass die Bewohner von Miami Wildtiere fangen. Also ist der Satz _____.

Tipp

Satz d): Du hast gelernt, dass Zahlen auf verschiedene Weisen ausgedrückt werden können. Entspricht die Jahreszahl aus dem Text *(in 1928)* der Angabe in der Aufgabe *(in the 19th century)*? Hier hilft dir dein Weltwissen: 1928 war im …

☐ 18. Jh.   ☐ 19. Jh.   ☐ 20. Jh.

Auswahlaufgabe mit Satzanfängen (Multiple choice)

Complete the sentences by choosing the correct ending according to the text. Write down the correct answers. Example: 4) – B)

1) The wildlife of the Everglades ...

A ☐ can be seen from the water and the land.

B ☐ is dangerous to visitors.

C ☐ includes snakes, alligators and dogs.

2) The water in the Everglades is polluted by ...

A ☐ rubbish left behind by the visitors.

B ☐ dirty water from a city.

C ☐ dead animals in lakes and rivers.

Tipp

Die Antwort zu Aufgabe 1) findest du im ersten Abschnitt. Doch dieser Abschnitt enthält einige Wörter, die du wahrscheinlich nicht kennst. Wie kommst du trotzdem auf die richtige Lösung?

1. **Ausschlussverfahren:** Hunde werden im ganzen Text nicht erwähnt. Haustiere werden zwar genannt, aber als Gefahr für die wilden Tiere. Also scheidet Lösung ____ wohl aus.

2. **Wortfamilien:** Das Wort *sight* aus dem Abschnitt kennst du nur als Sehenswürdigkeit in Städten. Das macht hier keinen Sinn. Doch steckt darin das Wort „sehen": *see*. Schau dir Lösung A also genauer an.

3. Der für Lösung A entscheidende Satz enthält weitere Wörter, die du wahrscheinlich nicht kennst, z. B. *specially-provided* und *trails*. Aber *airboat* und *hiking* dürftest du verstehen. Das eine tun die Touristen vom Wasser aus, das andere ...

3) The Everglades are drying out because ...

A ☐ of rising global temperatures.

B ☐ farmers use the water for their fields.

C ☐ the Highway cuts off the water from a part of the wetlands.

Tipp

3) Es geht hier ausschließlich um das, was im Text steht. Vielleicht hat das Austrocknen der Everglades mehrere Ursachen, die womöglich auch in den Lösungen A–C erwähnt werden. Aber im Text genannt wird nur eine davon, und die musst du auswählen.

4. Leseverstehen – *Now you*

In diesem Kapitel kannst du die Strategien, die du auf den letzten Seiten kennen gelernt hast, bei ausgewählten Aufgaben zum Leseverstehen gezielt üben. Grundlage dafür sind ein Artikel über die Filmindustrie in Neuseeland und ein Blog über ein Motorrad-Rennen auf der Isle of Man.

Filming in New Zealand

New Zealand's amazing nature has long attracted the world's top film directors.

The *Lord of the Rings* trilogy, for example, was filmed in different areas of New Zealand,
5 especially in the country's national parks. The films made use of spectacular mountains such as Mount Ngauruhoe, a treeless live volcano, and of rivers, lakes and wild canyons. But scenes were also filmed in the softer and less dramatic
10 green hills near Matamata.

One of the advantages of filming in New Zealand is the small number of people living there: only four and a half million people in a country more or less the same size as the United
15 Kingdom (population 64 million). So there are fewer buildings to ruin the views of open countryside.

Disney's movie *Pete's Dragon*, for example, needed huge redwood trees and a wild river
20 where a bear could scare the hero. This, too, was filmed in New Zealand. The wonderfully named Whakarewarewa Forest near Rotorua has Californian redwood trees and the McLaren Falls Park has the wild river. And a helicopter
25 company based in Queenstown helped to film the dragon as it flew over the mountains – not

Mount Ngauruhoe was used to represent the place where the ring was destroyed

the only example of how filming brings employment to more than only actors and producers.

Indeed, many of the visual effects that
30 make the dragon seem so real were created in offices in Wellington, New Zealand's capital and second largest city – which has itself played a role in a number of films. In the movie *King Kong*, for example, many of the scenes supposedly set
35 in New York were actually filmed in Wellington. This means that the southernmost capital city in the world has its own booming film industry with highly qualified professionals. After all, they have worked with some leading film
40 directors in the world.

Überschriften zuordnen *(Matching)*

Read the text about the film industry in New Zealand. Match the letter of the headings with the correct number of the parts of the text. Write down the correct answers. Example: 5) – f)

1) lines 1–10   **a)** Few inhabitants   _____

2) lines 11–17   **b)** Filming from the air   _____

3) lines 18–28   **c)** The power of natural beauty   _____

4) lines 29–40   **d)** Know-how is king   _____

Auswahlaufgaben mit Satzanfängen *(Multiple choice)*

> Read the text again. Complete the sentences by choosing the correct ending according to the text. Write down the correct answers. Example: 5) – A)

1) *The Lord of the Rings* was filmed in ...

   A ☐ more than one region.

   B ☐ national parks only.

   C ☐ one part of New Zealand.

2) New Zealand's population is ...

   A ☐ bigger than that of the United Kingdom.

   B ☐ smaller than that of the United Kingdom.

   C ☐ about the same size as that of the United Kingdom.

3) The makers of *Pete's Dragon* used ...

   A ☐ helicopters.

   B ☐ a famous racing car.

   C ☐ unemployed actors.

4) Wellington is ...

   A ☐ New Zealand's biggest city.

   B ☐ more exciting than New York.

   C ☐ the place where *King Kong* was filmed.

Synonyme Textstellen *(Sentence parts that mean the same)*

> Find the corresponding sentence parts or sentences in the text that mean the same and write them down.

a) International movie makers love New Zealand for its awesome landscape.

_____

b) New Zealand's population is not large, which is great for making films.

_____

c) This shows how the movie business gives work to people both inside and outside the film industry.

_____

The Isle of Man TT race

The Isle of Man is a small island between Britain and Ireland. It is famous for its motorcycle racing. The text is from a blog written by a resident of the island.

I live on one of Europe's quietest islands – the Isle of Man, set in the Irish Sea about half-way between England and Ireland. We have beautiful unspoilt countryside, narrow country roads, and every May or June we have the TT
5 (Tourist Trophy) race. It's one of the most fa-mous motorcycle racing events in the world, and the amazing thing is that it takes place on about 50 kilometres of our narrow public lanes.

10 Every year the roads are closed to the public for a week of practice runs followed by a week of racing. That means two weeks of road chaos on the island, when it's hard for locals to get from one part of the island to another. A trip that
15 usually takes ten minutes can take half an hour or more.

The only way you can bring your motorbike is by ferry, and in 2015 about 36,000 fans travelled to the Isle of Man, bringing over 14,000
20 motorbikes with them – that is 17 % more than the year before.

The TT has run every year since 1907. Only during the First and Second World Wars there were no races. The TT race has not always been
25 popular with racers, however. Between 1907 and 2015 no less than 246 people have lost their lives

Tourist Trophy race, Isle of Man (2015)

during the event – 141 racers, and 105 spectators and other members of the public. As a result, the event was boycotted by a number of leading motorbike riders in the early 1970s. A number of 30 important sponsors kept away too.

The event is great for the island's economy, but not everybody likes it. I, for one, am not a motorbike fan, and I hate the crowds and the noise. But I have learned to live with it: I just 35 book my holidays while the racing takes place. That way, I can get away from the chaos of the races and enjoy the sun in Turkey or Spain. And the best thing is that I can pay for my holiday by renting out my little house to people who come 40 to watch the TT race.

Überschriften zuordnen *(Matching)*

Read the blog about the TT race. Match the letter of the headings with the correct number of the parts of the text.

Write down the correct answers. Example: 6) – f)

1) lines 1–9   **a)** What is the TT race?   _____

2) lines 10–16   **b)** Escape   _____

3) lines 17–21   **c)** All by boat   _____

4) lines 22–31   **d)** Dangers   _____

5) lines 32–41   **e)** Difficult to move around   _____

Richtig-/Falsch-Aufgaben *(True, false or not in the text?)*

> Read the text again. Decide whether the statements are 'true', 'false' or 'not in the text'.
>
> Write down the correct answers. Example: f) – true

a) The motorbikes race on a specially made track. _____

b) During the race, many roads on the island can't be used. _____

c) More motorbike riders came to the island in 2015 than in 2014. _____

d) More racers have died in the TT race than in any other motorbike race. _____

e) In the early 1970s there were no TT races. _____

Teil C: *Use of language* (Wortschatz und Grammatik)

1. Ablauf und Bewertung

In der Regel bearbeitest du Prüfungsteil C *(Use of language)* im Anschluss an Prüfungsteil B *(Text-based tasks)*. Für die Prüfungsteile B, C und D *(Writing)* hast du zusammengenommen 90 Minuten Zeit, die du dir frei einteilen kannst. Plane also genügend Zeit für jeden Prüfungsteil ein und bedenke, dass du am Ende auch noch Zeit zum Korrekturlesen benötigst.

Teil C besteht aus fünf Teilen bzw. Aufgaben (Parts 1–5), die sich alle auf denselben Text beziehen:

- Lücken im Text füllen: Für jede Lücke gibt es drei mögliche Wörter und du musst entscheiden, welches inhaltlich und grammatikalisch am besten passt *(Fill in the gap, Multiple choice)*.
- zu vorgegebenen Wörtern das Gegenteil im Text finden *(Find the opposites)*
- zu vorgegebenen Wörtern Synonyme im Text finden *(Find the synonyms)*
- vorgegebene Wörter aus dem Text erklären *(Give a definition)*
- Fragen zum Text formulieren *(Asking questions)*

Du kannst beim Leseverstehen 15 Punkte erreichen. Damit wird dieser Prüfungsteil am wenigsten stark gewichtet.

Wie schon beim Leseverstehen, so darfst du auch in Prüfungsteil C ein zweisprachiges Wörterbuch verwenden. Bei schweren Fehlern in der Grammatik oder Rechtschreibung verlierst du einen ganzen Punkt, bei leichteren Fehlern einen halben Punkt. Schreibst du mehr Lösungen auf als gefordert, so verlierst du ebenfalls Punkte.

2. Aufgabenformate in Baden-Württemberg

In diesem Kapitel lernst du beispielhaft die wichtigsten Aufgabenformate kennen, die dir beim Hauptschulabschluss in Baden-Württemberg im Bereich *Use of language* begegnen können.

Die Tipp-Kästen enthalten nützliche Strategien, wie du mit häufigen Schwierigkeiten umgehen kannst.

Auswahlaufgaben mit Lücken *(Fill in the gap, Multiple choice)*

Du bekommst einen Text mit Lücken, die du füllen musst. Für jede Lücke gibt es drei Vorschläge und du musst den inhaltlich und grammatikalisch passenden Vorschlag auswählen. In der Prüfung sind es in der Regel sechs Lücken, hier sind es zu Übungszwecken mehr.

> Read the text and find the correct word.
>
> Write down the correct word.

My new job

Most parents give their (_____**a)**_____) pocket money.

Mine give me money too, but it's never enough for what I need.

So I looked (_____**b)**_____) jobs in our town. But when I finally

(_____**c)**_____) a job in a clothes shop, my parents (_____**d)**_____)

happy at all.

They say that if I have a job, I'll be too (_____ **e)** _____) for school and for doing my homework, even though no teacher has ever complained about my school work. They say that the music in the shop is louder (_____ **f)** _____) it should be. They say that the shop sells cheap clothes that were (_____ **g)** _____) in Bangladesh, where people often work in terrible conditions for very little pay. They would prefer it, they say, if I (_____ **h)** _____) in a Fairtrade shop that sends money back to the workers _____ **i)** _____) make the products.

Tipp

Bei Verben – hier Lücken **c)**, **d)**, **g)** und **h)** – überlege immer:

- Welche Zeitform *(tense)*?
- Aktiv oder Passiv?
- Einzahl oder Mehrzahl?
- Bejaht oder verneint?
- Regelmäßig oder unregelmäßig?
- *-s* im *simple present* bei *he/she/it*

a)	children	children's	child's	_____
b)	after	for	forward	_____
c)	find	found	founded	_____
d)	weren't	were	won't	_____
e)	able	proud	tired	_____
f)	when	then	than	_____
g)	sold	made	done	_____
h)	worked	working	works	_____
i)	where	who	the	_____

Tipp

a)	Vorsicht: unregelmäßige Pluralform!
b)	Nach *look* können verschiedene Präpositionen stehen. Welche passt hier zur Bedeutung „suchen"?
e)	Welches Adjektiv macht hier am meisten Sinn?
f)	Bei einem Vergleich (Komparativ) brauchst du welches Wort?
h)	Achtung, *if*-Satz! Im Hauptsatz steht *would*, also brauchst du hier welche Form?
i)	Das gesuchte Wort bezieht sich auf *workers*, also auf Personen …

Gegensätze finden *(Find the opposites)*

Bei diesem Aufgabenformat sollst du zu vorgegebenen Wörtern die Gegensätze *(opposites)* im Text finden.

In der Regel werden in der Prüfung zwei Wörter vorgegeben, hier sind es zu Übungszwecken mehr.

Tipp

Zu einigen Wörtern gibt es nur wenige Gegensätze oder Synonyme. Es lohnt sich daher, eine Liste anzulegen, auf der du alle Gegensätze und Synonyme notierst. Vielleicht kommen ja einige Wörter aus deiner Liste bei der Prüfung dran!

Indian food in Britain

Indian cooking has been popular in Britain for longer than many people realize: a British cookery book in 1774 contained numerous recipes for Indian dishes. Many British people were familiar with Indian food because Britain governed India, and a huge number of British people lived there.

5

In the early 20th century, more and more Indian seamen reached Britain's shores. Many decided to stay and run small restaurants. The men were often from areas in Bangladesh and Pakistan. This was all part of British India back then, so the food was called Indian food. The cafe owners soon noticed that people returning from late shifts at work wanted to buy hot food before getting the bus home. They did not have time to sit down and eat; they wanted their meals in a form that they could carry. This was the birth of the *Indian take-away*.

10

15

While for years *chicken tikka masala* was the best-selling dish served in Indian take-aways, customers are now trying out a wider range of dishes. One reason for this is the enormous influence of TV food programmes and food blogs: customers are now more informed about the range of food available. It also reflects people's concerns about their own health, with many customers looking for lower-calorie dishes.

20

25

Find the opposites in the text. Write down the correct answer.

a) few — *many*

b) died — *lived*

c) late — *early*

d) less — *more*

e) leave — *stay*

f) women — *men*

g) sell — *buy*

h) after — *before*

i) get up — *sit down*

j) drink — *eat*

k) narrower — *wider*

l) unavailable — *available*

m) higher — *lower*

Tipp

Manche Gegensätze werden mit Vorsilben wie *im-*, *un-* oder *dis-* gebildet, z. B.:

happy ⟷ *unhappy*

possible ⟷ *impossible*

agree ⟷ *disagree*

Manchmal ist das Gegenteil aber auch ein völlig anderes Wort, z. B.:

big ⟷ *small*

love ⟷ *hate*

Merke dir die unregelmäßigen Adjektive und Adverbien:

better ⟷ *worse*

badly ⟷ *well*

Tipp

Das Wort, das du im Text finden sollst, hat meist dieselbe Form wie das vorgegebene Wort, z. B.:
died in **b)** ist eine Form des *simple past* → Such im Text eine Form im *simple past*.
narrower in **k)** ist eine Steigerungsform → Such im Text eine Steigerungsform.

Wörter mit der gleichen Bedeutung finden *(Find the synonyms)*

Als nächstes sollst du zu vorgegebenen Wörtern Synonyme im Text finden. Synonyme sind Wörter mit der gleichen oder einer sehr ähnlichen Bedeutung.

In der Regel werden in der Prüfung zwei Wörter vorgegeben, hier sind es zu Übungszwecken mehr.

> **Tipp**
>
> Wenn du das passende Wort im Text gefunden hast, setze das vorgegebene Wort aus der Aufgabe probehalber in den Text ein: Passt es von der Wortart und von der Bedeutung her?

> Read the text about Indian food again. Find the synonyms in the text. Write down the correct answer.

a) many   *numerous*

b) large   *huge*

c) little   *small*

d) regions   *areas*

e) coming back   *returning*

f) catching   *getting*

g) beginning   *birth*

h) great   *enormous*

> **Tipp**
>
> Achte auch hier immer auf die Wortart und die Form. Beispiel:
>
> Das vorgegebene Wort *regions* in **d)** ist ein Nomen in der Mehrzahl. → Such im Text ein Nomen in der Mehrzahl!
>
> Das vorgegebene Wort *beginning* in **g)** kann dagegen ein Verb in der *ing*-Form oder ein Nomen sein → Such im Text nach Nomen oder *irg*-Formen!
>
> Das Synonym eines Wortes kann auch aus einer anderen Anzahl an Wörtern bestehen. Beispiel: In **e)** ist *coming back* vorgegeben, also ein Verb, das aus zwei Wörtern besteht. Es kann aber durchaus sein, dass das Synonym im Text nur aus einem Wort besteht!

Wörter erklären *(Give a definition)*

Bei diesem Format geht es darum, Wörter aus dem Text zu erklären. Du erhältst in der Regel drei Wörter zur Auswahl und sollst dir zwei davon aussuchen, die du dann in deinen eigenen Worten definierst.

Hier sind es zu Übungszwecken mehr.

> Choose **five** of the following words from the text and give a definition.

a) contain (line 3):

_____

_____

b) govern (line 6):

_____

_____

> **Tipp**
>
> Versuche, dir den Sinn unbekannter Wörter zu erschließen:
>
> *contain* in **a)** kennst du vielleicht nicht – aber Container ist dir wahrscheinlich ein Begriff!
>
> *govern* in **b)** ist dir vielleicht neu, aber erinnerst du dich noch an das Wort *government* aus der gleichen Wortfamilie?

c) century (line 8):

_____

_____

d) restaurant (line 10):

_____

_____

e) best-selling (line 21):

_____

_____

f) customer (line 22):

_____

_____

g) blog (line 25):

_____

_____

Fragen zum Text formulieren _(Asking questions)_

Bei diesem Aufgabenformat sollst du Fragen zum Text stellen. Die Fragen müssen sich voneinander unterscheiden. Mische also Fragen mit Fragewort und Fragen ohne Fragewort. Wiederhole vorher noch einmal die Bildung von Fragen, z. B. anhand der interaktiven Übungen auf www.scook.de.

> You want to know more about Indian food in Britain. Ask three questions.

1) _____ ?

2) _____ ?

3) _____ ?

Teil D: *Writing* (Schreiben)

1. Ablauf und Bewertung

In der Regel bearbeitest du Prüfungsteil D *(Writing)* im Anschluss an die Prüfungsteile B *(Text-based tasks)* und C *(Use of language)*. Für die Prüfungsteile B, C und D hast du zusammengenommen 90 Minuten Zeit, die du dir frei einteilen kannst. Plane also genügend Zeit für jeden Prüfungsteil ein und bedenke, dass du am Ende auch noch Zeit zum Korrekturlesen benötigst.

Teil D besteht aus zwei Schreibaufgaben (Parts 1 und 2):
- **Korrespondenz:** Bei der kürzeren ersten Schreibaufgabe (mindestens 60 Wörter) erstellst du einen Brief oder eine E-Mail. Dir wird ein Szenario vorgegeben und du erhältst einige inhaltliche Vorgaben, die du berücksichtigen sollst (bestimmte Fragen stellen, dich beschweren, von etwas berichten etc.).
- **freies Schreiben:** In der längeren zweiten Schreibaufgabe (ungefähr 80 Wörter) sollst du von Erlebnissen, Erfahrungen oder Vorlieben berichten oder deine Meinung äußern. Als Unterstützung erhältst du auch einige Ideen oder Redemittel, die du aber nicht alle verwenden musst.

Du kannst beim Schreiben 20 Punkte erreichen (Part 1: 8 Punkte, Part 2: 12 Punkte). Die Punkte bekommst du, wenn du alle inhaltlichen Vorgaben der Aufgabenstellung berücksichtigst. Bei schweren Fehlern in der Grammatik oder Rechtschreibung können dir aber auch Punkte abgezogen werden, bei leichteren Fehlern auch halbe Punkte. Wie schon bei den Prüfungsteilen B und C, darfst du auch in Prüfungsteil D ein zweisprachiges Wörterbuch verwenden.

2. Aufgabenformate in Baden-Württemberg

In diesem Kapitel lernst du beispielhaft die wichtigsten Aufgabenformate kennen, die dir beim Hauptschulabschluss in Baden-Württemberg im Bereich *Writing* begegnen können.

Die Tipp-Kästen enthalten nützliche Strategien, wie du mit häufigen Schwierigkeiten umgehen kannst.

Erste (kürzere) Schreibaufgabe: Korrespondenz

Bei der ersten Schreibaufgabe sollst du einen Brief oder eine E-Mail verfassen. Es kann dir eine E-Mail vorgegeben werden, die du beantworten sollst, oder eine Situation oder ein Thema, zu dem du dich in Form eines Briefes oder einer E-Mail äußern sollst. In jedem Fall erhältst du einige Inhaltspunkte, von denen du einige erwähnen und ausarbeiten musst. Außerdem wird von dir erwartet, dass du eine passende Anrede und eine passende Grußformel für dein Schreiben findest.

1. Persönliche Briefe oder E-Mails

Die Prüfungsaufgabe kann zum Beispiel so aussehen:

Ava is an English student who is going to join your class next year. Your English teacher has asked you to write Ava an email giving information about your town.

Include **at least 3** of the following points:

- interesting places
- activities for teenagers
- ideas for weekends
- questions for Ava

Write at least 60 words.

Schritt 1: Lies die Arbeitsanweisung genau durch und markiere Schlüsselwörter. Du musst mindestens drei Inhaltspunkte berücksichtigen, sonst kannst du nicht die volle Punktzahl erhalten. Markiere daher die Inhaltspunkte, für die du dich entscheidest.

Schritt 2: Mach dir klar, wer der Empfänger ist, und wähle die richtige Anrede und Grußformel. Fülle zur Wiederholung folgende Tabelle aus:

Tipp

Schau in dein Englischbuch, falls du diese Redemittel vergessen hast!

	Persönlicher Brief oder E-Mail	Formeller Brief oder E-Mail
Anrede	*Dear ...,* Hello hi	Dear sir and Madam / Mr /Mrs/M
Gruß	Yours, Love, Best wishes	Yours sincerly, yours faithfully

Schritt 3: Nun geht es an den Text selbst. Überlege dir eine Struktur und mache dir Notizen, z. B. in einem Network oder in einer Tabelle wie dieser. Die meisten Schreiben sind so gegliedert:

Einleitung	*I'm happy to hear that you will join ...* *Our teacher told us that ...*
Mittelteil	*Our town is really nice/special/... because ...* *– Places:* *–*
Schluss	*When/Where/What/...?* *Do/Are/Have you ...?*

Schritt 4: Wie könnte deine Lösung aussehen? Hier ist ein Beispiel. Einiges ist darin gut, z. B. hat es eine Anrede und einen Gruß, und es sind drei Inhaltspunkte berücksichtigt *(places, activities, questions)*. Aber Achtung: Die blau markierten Wörter sind fehlerhaft. Lies die Hinweise in den Kästen und verbessere die Fehler.

Tipp

Mit diesem Beispiel kannst du üben, deinen fertigen Text gründlich durchzulesen und auf Fehler zu überprüfen.

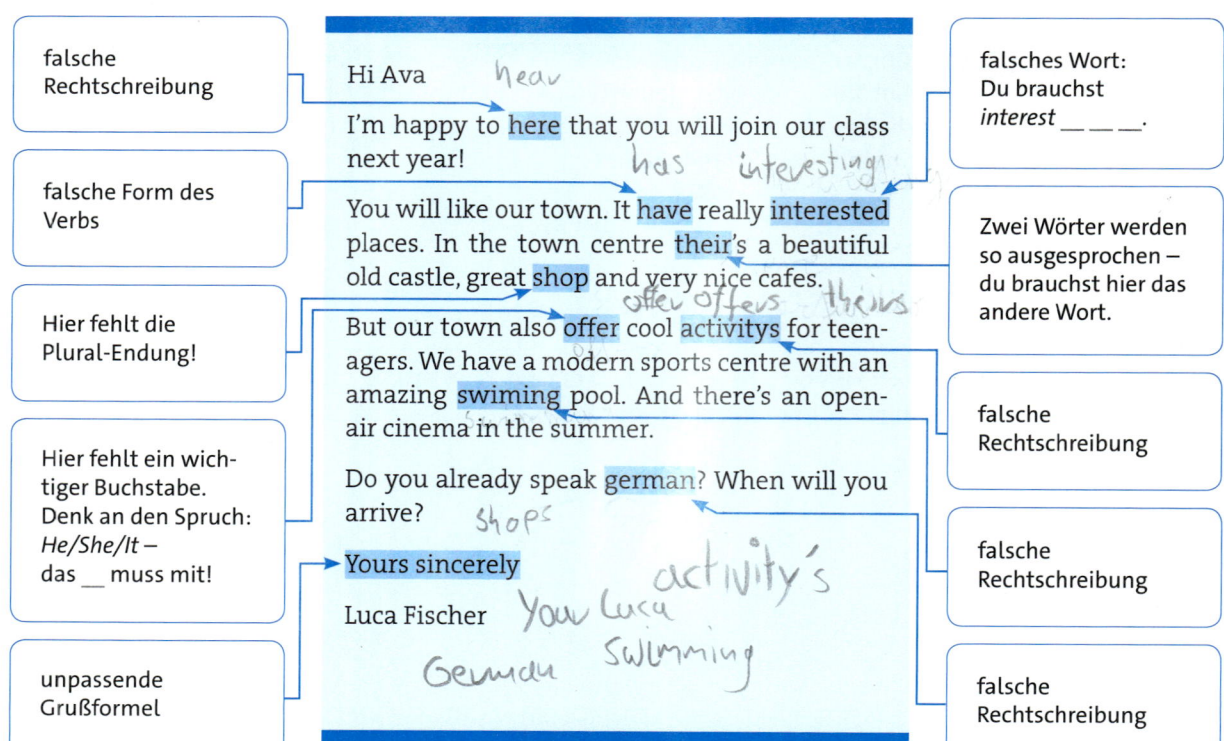

falsche Rechtschreibung

falsche Form des Verbs

Hier fehlt die Plural-Endung!

Hier fehlt ein wichtiger Buchstabe. Denk an den Spruch: *He/She/It –* das __ muss mit!

unpassende Grußformel

falsches Wort: Du brauchst *interest* _ _ _.

Zwei Wörter werden so ausgesprochen – du brauchst hier das andere Wort.

falsche Rechtschreibung

falsche Rechtschreibung

falsche Rechtschreibung

Tipp

Schau dir noch einmal deine letzten drei Klassenarbeiten an. Erstelle eine Checkliste mit acht bis zehn Fehlern, die mehrmals aufgetaucht sind. Beispiel:

wrong:	right:
~~I not like this.~~	I don't like this.

Sieh dir diese Liste immer wieder an, um diese Fehler in Zukunft zu vermeiden.

Schritt 5: Jetzt bist du dran! Schreibe deine E-Mail an Ava gemäß Aufgabenstellung. Denke daran, dass du mindestens drei der vier Inhaltspunkte aus der Aufgabenstellung berücksichtigen musst.

Tipp

Es ist immer leichter, Fehler bei anderen zu finden! Daher ist es eine gute Übung, Texte von einem Partner oder einer Partnerin zu überprüfen.

Schritt 6: Überprüfe deinen Text zum Schluss immer auf Fehler – auch in der Prüfung, sonst kannst du Punkte verlieren!

Diese Checklisten können dir helfen:

Prüfe, ob du die Aufgabenstellung erfüllt hast:	
Hast du eine passende Anrede geschrieben?	☐
Hast du mindestens drei Inhaltspunkte berücksichtigt?	☐
Hast du eine klare Struktur mit Absätzen verwendet?	☐
Hast du eine passende Grußformel verwendet?	☐
Hast du mindestens 60 Wörter geschrieben?	☐

Prüfe auch die Sprache:	
Stimmen die Zeitformen der Verben?	☐
Stimmen die Verneinungen?	☐
Hast du Wörter, bei deren Rechtschreibung du unsicher bist, im Wörterbuch überprüft?	☐
Stimmt die Satzstellung (Subjekt – Verb – Objekt)?	☐
Hast du an das -s nach *he/she/it* gedacht?	☐
Hast du an das -s beim Plural gedacht?	☐

2. Formelle Briefe oder E-Mails

Es kann auch sein, dass du in der Prüfung ein formelles Schreiben verfassen musst. Typische Beispiele sind Beschwerden oder die Bitte um Auskunft. Wieder erhältst du einige Inhaltspunkte, die du erwähnen oder ausarbeiten sollst. Und natürlich musst du eine passende Anrede und eine passende Grußformel finden.

Schritt 1: Bei formellen E-Mails oder Briefen gibt es einige Besonderheiten, die du beachten solltest. Wiederhole die wichtigsten Regeln:

- Du wendest dich an jemanden, den du nicht oder kaum kennst. Daher sollte dein Stil höflich sein.
- Es gibt einige typische Redewendungen vor allem für die Anrede und den Gruß, die du dir einprägen solltest. Fülle zur Wiederholung diese Tabelle aus:

Formelle E-Mails oder Briefe		
	Name des Empfängers bekannt	**Name des Empfängers unbekannt**
Anrede	*Dear Mr/Mrs/Ms (+ name)*	*Dear* Sir *or* Madame
Gruß	*Yours* Sincerely *(mit freundlichen grüßen)* *Yours* faithfully *(Hochachtungsvoll)*
	Etwas weniger formeller Gruß: *Regards, Best wishes*	

- Verwende nicht die Kurzform der Verben, sondern ihre Langform, z. B.:

nicht: ~~I'd like to apply ...~~   sondern: *I would like to apply ...*

nicht: ~~I'm very reliable ...~~   sondern: _____

nicht: ~~It's broken and ...~~   sondern: _____

nicht: ~~I'll return ...~~   sondern: _____

nicht: It ~~didn't work~~ ...   sondern: _____

nicht: ~~You've sent~~ ...   sondern: _____

Schritt 2: Schau dir zwei typische Prüfungsaufgaben an und bearbeite die Aufgaben zu den Lösungsbeispielen:

a) **Beschwerdebrief:** Lies die Prüfungsaufgabe und fülle die Lücken im Lösungsbeispiel auf Seite 37 mit Wortschatz aus dem Kasten.

> You ordered a new phone online, but there were some problems. Write an email and complain.
>
> Include **at least 3** of the following points:
>
> - delivery
> - missing or broken parts
> - customer service
> - what you expect the company to do
>
> Write at least 60 words.

Dear [Sir or Madame]

I [Ordered] a phone [on] Friday 3rd May.

The delivery took much longer than [expectet].

When the phone finally [arrived] here, the front was [broken] and the phone did

not [work]. What is more, the charger was [missing].

I phoned your [customer service] many times, but unfortunately nobody answers.

I am very [unhappy] with this service.

Please can you [send] me a new phone and a charger. I will then [return] the

broken phone.

Many [thanks] for your [cooperation].

Yours [faithfully]

Callum Spencer

> faithfully • thanks • ordered •
> broken • work • return • send •
> cooperation • Sir or Madam • on •
> unhappy • arrived • missing •
> customer service • expected

b) **Bitte um Auskunft:** Lies die Prüfungsaufgabe. Im Lösungsbeispiel sind einige Sätze durcheinandergeraten. Bringe sie in die richtige Reihenfolge:

> You and your friends want to spend a week on a campsite in Scotland. Write an email and ask for information.
>
> Include **at least 3** of the following points:
>
> • prices • transport • food • activities
>
> Write at least 60 words.

Dear Sir or Madam

I have read about your campsite on your website, but I have a few questions.

Can you please / for three people / tell me / with a tent / what the price is / per night / ?

Can you please *tell me what the price is for three people per night?*

Can we / or is there / walk to / the station / a bus from / the campsite / ?

Can we walk to a bus from the station or is there the campsite

Is there / can buy / where / bread, milk, etc. / we / a shop / ?

Is there a shop where we can buy bread, milk, etc?

Thank you / in advance / very much / for your help / .

Thank you very much For you help in advance

Yours faithfully

Amal Ghali

Schritt 3: Verbindungswörter *(linking words)* helfen dem Leser, deinen Text besser zu verstehen. Das folgende Beispiel für eine Beschwerdemail enthält keine Verbindungswörter und liest sich daher nicht gut. Lies die Prüfungsaufgabe und verbessere den Text, indem du die Verbindungswörter im Kasten einsetzt:

You spent a few nights in a hotel with your parents, but there were some problems with your room. Write an email and complain.

Include **at least 3** of the following points:

- bathroom
- missing or broken things
- noise
- view

Write at least 60 words.

Dear Ms Smith

We stayed in your hotel from 1st to 5th May.

We were very unhappy with our room.

The bathroom was dirty.

There were no towels.

It was very noisy. People were drinking in front of the hotel all night.

We didn't get any sleep.

Your website promised a view of the sea. We couldn't see the sea.

We would like to get a full refund.

I look forward to hearing from you soon.

Yours sincerely

Zoe Turner

Tipp

Anrede von Frauen in formellen Briefen:

Mrs wurde früher für verheiratete Frauen verwendet, *Miss* für unverheiratete. Beide Anreden sind heute nicht mehr so üblich.

Ms ist eine neutrale Anrede für alle Frauen und passt immer!

Tipp

Wiederhole vor der Prüfung die Schreibweise der Daten auf Englisch, z.B. anhand des Kastens auf Seite 56. Dies kann dir beim Verfassen formeller Schreiben nützen.

Then • So now • But • As a result • but • because • What's more • And finally • To begin with

---

Schritt 4: Jetzt bist du dran! Lies die Prüfungsaufgabe und schreibe deinen Brief.

You had lunch in a restaurant in London, and it was not a good experience. Write a letter to the restaurant and complain.

Include **at least 3** of the following points:

- the food
- the service
- other guests
- what you expect now

Write at least 60 words.

► Fortsetzung (S. 39) nach den Lösungen

Englisch

ABSCHLUSS-PRÜFUNGS-TRAINER

Hauptschulabschluss
Baden-Württemberg

Lösungen

Auswahlaufgaben mit Fragen *(Multiple choice)*

Short conversations

a) B · b) A · c) B

Auswahlaufgaben mit Satzanfängen *(Multiple choice)*

A visit to Krakow

a) B · b) C · c) A · d) B · e) C

Notizen in einer Tabelle anfertigen *(Fill in the table)*

A tourist attraction in Brighton

a) August 2016
b) 11 million
c) 360-degree view of town below / a great view / a view of the town below / …
d) London
e) £15 / 15 pounds

Zuordnungsaufgaben *(Matching)*

Skyways in the US and Canada

a) F · b) D · c) A · d) G · e) B

Auswahlaufgaben mit Satzanfängen *(Multiple choice)*

The Niagara Falls (Part 1)

1. a) C · b) A
2. a) mainly · b) waterproof ponchos

Auswahlaufgaben mit Fragen *(Multiple choice)*

The Niagara Falls (Part 2)

1. a) C · b) B
2. and taken care of

Notizen in einer Tabelle anfertigen *(Fill in the table)*

The Niagara Falls (Part 3)

1. a) 1901 · b) 63 · c) money · d) head
2. a) raise money · b) was bleeding

Auswahlaufgaben mit Satzanfängen und Fragen *(Multiple choice)*

Two fantastic cycle races

a) C · b) C · c) B · d) A · e) B

Notizen in einer Tabelle anfertigen *(Fill in the table)*

Bob Marley

a) in Jamaica in 1945
b) Sussex/England
c) mother
d) The Teenagers
e) Buffalo Soldier / I shot the Sheriff / No Woman, No Cry / Concrete Jungle

Auswahlaufgaben mit Erklärungen *(Multiple choice)*

Understanding signs

a) B · b) C · c) A · d) C · e) A

Überschriften zuordnen *(Matching)*

Australia's Stolen Generations

1) lines 1–5: b)
2) lines 6–8: c)
3) lines 9–13: a)
4) lines 14–18: d)

Richtig-/Falsch-Aufgaben *(True, false or not in the text?)*

Australia's Stolen Generations

a) true · b) false · c) not in the text · d) true

Auswahlaufgaben mit Satzanfängen *(Multiple choice)*

Kasun's first day at a new school

1) B · 2) A · 3) C · 4) B

Synonyme Textstellen *(Sentence parts that mean the same)*

Kasun's first day at a new school

a) … I was scared stiff.
b) … my knees were like jelly.
c) Her red eyes told their own story.
d) … I felt like a fish out of water.

Überschriften zuordnen *(Matching)*

The Everglades

1) lines 1–7: b)
2) lines 8–12: a)
3) lines 13–21: d)
4) lines 22–25: c)

Richtig-/Falsch-Aufgaben *(True, false or not in the text?)*

The Everglades

a) false · b) not in the text · c) true · d) false · e) false

Auswahlaufgaben mit Satzanfängen *(Multiple choice)*

The Everglades

1) A · 2) B · 3) C

Überschriften zuordnen *(Matching)*

Filming in New Zealand

1) lines 1–10: c)
2) lines 11–17: a)
3) lines 18–28: b)
4) lines 29–40: d)

Auswahlaufgaben mit Satzanfängen *(Multiple choice)*

Filming in New Zealand

1) A · 2) B · 3) A · 4) C

Synonyme Textstellen *(Sentence parts that mean the same)*

Filming in New Zealand

a) New Zealand's amazing nature has long attracted the world's top film directors.

b) One of the advantages of filming in New Zealand is the small number of people living there.

c) … – not the only example of how filming brings employment to more than only actors and producers.

Überschriften zuordnen *(Matching)*

The Isle of Man TT race
1) lines 1–9: a)
2) lines 10–16: e)
3) lines 17–21: c)
4) lines 22–31: d)
5) lines 32–41: b)

Richtig-/Falsch-Aufgaben *(True, false or not in the text?)*

The Isle of Man TT race
a) false · b) true · c) true · d) not in the text · e) false

TRAINING SECTION, Teil C: *Use of language* ▶ p. 28–32

Auswahlaufgaben mit Lücken *(Fill in the gap, Multiple choice)*

My new job
a) children · b) for · c) found · d) weren't · e) tired · f) than · g) made · h) worked · i) who

Gegensätze finden *(Find the opposites)*

Indian food in Britain
a) many (line 2) · b) lived (line 7) · c) early (line 8) · d) more (line 8) · e) stay (line 10) · f) men (line 11) · g) buy (line 15) · h) before (line 16) · i) sit down (line 17) · j) eat (line 17) · k) wider (line 22) · l) available (line 26) · m) lower (line 29)

Wörter mit der gleichen Bedeutung finden *(Find the synonyms)*

Indian food in Britain
a) numerous (line 3) · b) huge (line 6) · c) small (line 10) · d) areas (line 11) · e) returning (line 14) · f) getting (line 16) · g) birth (line 19) · h) enormous (line 24)

Wörter erklären *(Give a definition)*

Indian food in Britain
Lösungsbeispiel:

a) If something contains things, those things are inside it. / to have something inside /…

b) to rule / to control a country / to be in charge of a country / to make the laws in a country / to have the power in a country /…

c) a (period of) hundred years

d) a place where you eat and pay for your meal / a business where food is served /…

e) selling in very large numbers / something that is bought very often /…

f) a person who buys something

g) a website where someone regularly writes about his/her thoughts or experiences / an online platform on which people write about their lives /…

Fragen zum Text formulieren *(Asking questions)*
Lösungsbeispiel:

Is Indian food healthier than English or German food?
Did Indian food change when it came to England?
What does 'tikka masala' mean?
What other dishes except for *chicken tikka masala* are there?
Do British families also cook Indian food at home?
Are there still all the small restaurants in Britain?

TRAINING SECTION, Teil D: *Writing* ▶ p. 33–43

Erste (kürzere) Schreibaufgabe: Korrespondenz

1. Persönliche Briefe oder E-Mails

Schritt 2

	Persönlicher Brief oder E-Mail	Formeller Brief oder E-Mail
Anrede	Dear …, Hi …, Hello … (+ name)	Dear Mr/Mrs/Ms (+ name) Dear Sir or Madam
Gruß	Bye for now / Yours / Best wishes / Love / Yours / Regards /…	Yours sincerely Yours faithfully

Schritt 3
Lösungsbeispiel:

Einleitung	I'm happy to hear that you will join our class next year. Our teacher told us that you would like to hear about our town.
Mittelteil	Our town is really nice/special/… because … – Places: parks, sightseeing, cafes, … – Activities: theatre, museum, cinema, ice skating, … – …
Schluss	When will you arrive? /… Where do you want to go first? / … What are your hobbies? / … Do you have any questions? / … Are you looking forward to seeing our town? / … Have you been to our town before? / …

Schritt 4
here: hear · have: has · interested: interesting · their's: there's · shop: shops · offer: offers · activitys: activities · swiming: swimming · german: German · Yours sincerely: See you soon /…

Schritt 5
Lösungsbeispiel:

Dear Ava

I'm Max from Berlin. Our teacher told us that you will join our class next year.

Berlin is a great city. There are always things to do. You can go to the cinema, a nice cafe or a cool shop. If you prefer to be outside, you can always hang out in one of the many parks or go swimming in a lake.

What are your hobbies? Would you like to know more about Berlin?

See you soon
Max

(80 Wörter)

2. Formelle Briefe oder E-Mails

Schritt 1

	Name des Empfängers bekannt	Name des Empfängers unbekannt
Anrede	Dear Mr/Mrs/Ms (+ name)	Dear Sir or Madam
Gruß	Yours sincerely	Yours faithfully

I would like to apply ...
I am very reliable ...
It is broken and ...
I will return ...
It did not work ...
You have sent ...

Schritt 2
a)

Dear Sir or Madam

I ordered a phone on Friday 3rd May. The delivery took much longer than expected.

When the phone finally arrived here, the front was broken and the phone did not work. What is more, the charger was missing.

I phoned your customer service many times, but unfortunately nobody answers. I am very unhappy with this service.

Please can you send me a new phone and a charger. I will then return the broken phone.

Many thanks for your cooperation.

Yours faithfully

Callum Spencer

b)
Can you please tell me what the price is for three people with a tent per night? / Can you please tell me what the price is per night for three people with a tent?
Can we walk to the campsite or is there a bus from the station?
Is there a shop where we can buy bread, milk, etc.?
Thank you very much in advance for your help.

Schritt 3

Dear Ms Smith

We stayed in your hotel from 1st to 5th May. But we were very unhappy with our room.

To begin with, the bathroom was dirty. Then, there were no towels. What's more, it was very noisy because people were drinking in front of the hotel all night. As a result, we didn't get any sleep. And finally, your website promised a view of the sea, but we couldn't see the sea.

So now we would like to get a full refund.

I look forward to hearing from you soon.

Yours sincerely

Zoe Turner

Schritt 4
Lösungsbeispiel:

Dear Sir or Madam

On Thursday 26th March my parents and I had lunch in your restaurant and it was not a good experience.

My father ordered fish but got sausages, my mother's potatoes were cold and my steak was grey. When we complained about this, the waiter was very unfriendly. He told us that he was busy.

We would now like to get the money back that we paid for this meal.

Yours faithfully
Senada Jupic

(75 Wörter)

Zweite (längere) Schreibaufgabe: Erlebnisse, Erfahrungen, Meinungen, Vorlieben

1. Über Erfahrungen und Erlebnisse schreiben

Schritt 1

a) Inhalt:
Where: mountains, Black Forest
When: last autumn
Who: I, cousin Charlie
Why special: adventures: cooking on an open fire / on top of highest mountain in Black Forest / meeting new people / ...
What: hiking / trip in the mountains
How: with tent and backpack / bad weather / ...

b) Sprache
1.
simple past: went, was, hiked, climbed, cooked, wasn't, came out, didn't give up, talked, laughed, met, helped
simple present: I'm not, I'm, I think, I hope
will-future: I'll organize, will be (luckier)

2./3.
Adjektive: great, awful, muddy, steep, open, wet, amazing, highest, sporty, proud, nice, longer, luckier
Verbindungswörter: but, so, and
Zeitwörter: last autumn, in the evening, the next day, usually, next year

Schritt 2
Lösungsbeispiel:

Last year I went to New Zealand with my parents. It was a great trip.

First, we stayed on the North Island, which has beautiful beaches and interesting cities like Auckland and Wellington. Then we travelled to the South Island. The huge mountains were amazing! Our highlight was a trip over an icy mountain on a helicopter. It was also a bit scary.

I hope that I can go to New Zealand again to see all the places I haven't seen yet!

(84 Wörter)

2. Über Vorlieben schreiben, seine Meinung äußern

Schritt 2
Lösungsbeispiel:

My favourite TV programme is called *Tatort*.

It's a weekly crime series with different police teams in different cities. The teams have to solve a crime, usually a murder.
I like *Tatort* for three reasons: First, it's exciting and relaxing at the same time. Second, it sometimes plays in Cologne, so I know the streets and buildings. And third, it's a programme that the whole family can agree on.
So every Sunday evening we come together in our living room and watch *Tatort* together.

(84 Wörter)

TRAINING SECTION Kommunikationsprüfung ▶ p. 44–56

Teil 2: Dialogisches Sprechen

Schritte 1 und 2
Lösungsbeispiel:

	Frage	Antwort
when?	When does the club meet? When does it take place? What are the practice times?	The club meets on … at … / It takes place on … at … / They practise on … at … / …
where?	Where does the club meet? Where do you practise? Where does it take place?	The club meets at the gym. / Practice is at the gym. / It takes place at the gym. / …
costs?	How much does it cost? How much do I have to pay? What are the costs?	It doesn't cost anything. / It costs nothing. / It's free! / You don't have to pay. / …
clothes?	What do I have to wear? What do I have to bring? Do I have to wear special clothes?	You should wear comfortable clothes. / You have to bring/wear comfortable clothes. / Nothing special, just comfortable clothes.

	Frage	Antwort
information?	Where can I get further information? Who can tell me more? Who do I contact for more information?	You can get further information if you contact Kevin. / You can call Kevin or send him an email. / You can contact Kevin. / … His phone number is: … His email address is: …

Teil 3: Sprachmittlung

Schritt 1
Lösungsbeispiel:

Adelola: I'd like to know if boys and girls play together in mixed teams.

You: Das Mädchen / Sie möchte wissen, ob Jungs und Mädchen zusammen in gemischten Mannschaften spielen.

Coach: Zurzeit gibt es leider keine gemischten Mannschaften.

You: There are no mixed teams at the moment.

Adelola: OK. But do you have a girls' team?

You: Gibt es denn eine Mädchenmannschaft?

Coach: Ja, wir haben eine Mannschaft für Mädchen zwischen 12 und 16 Jahren.

You: There's a team for girls between 12 and 16.

Adelola: That's great! And what are the practice times?

You: Wann sind die Trainingszeiten?

Coach: Die Mädchenmannschaft trainiert freitags um 16 Uhr. Sie kann gerne nächste Woche kommen.

You: The girls' team practises at 4 pm on Fridays. You can come next week.

Adelola: I will. Thank you so much!

Schritt 3
Lösungsbeispiel:

He has a sore throat. · Can you help him? · Can he pay by credit card? · He doesn't have any cash.

Du solltest viel trinken. · Sie nehmen/akzeptieren (leider) keine Kreditkarten. · Sie kann uns/dir zeigen, wo ein Geldautomat ist. · Ruf sie an, wenn du nächste Woche noch krank bist.

Schritt 4
Lösungsbeispiel:

Aedan: I lost my phone. Can you help me?

You: Er hat sein Handy verloren. Können Sie ihm helfen? / Wurde es hier vielleicht abgegeben?

Assistant: Ich brauche da mehr Details. Wann und wo hat er es verloren?

You: When and where did you lose it?

Aedan: I think it was at the smoothie stand, at around 6 pm.

You: Das war wohl am Smoothie-Stand, gegen 18 Uhr.

Assistant: Und wie sieht es aus?

You: What does it look like?

Aedan: It's a white Sumsang BX7. And it has stickers on the back.

You: Es ist ein weißes Sumsang BX7 mit Aufklebern auf der Rückseite.

Assistant: Er hat Glück. Das Handy ist hier. Ich gehe es holen.

You: It's here. He/She is going to get it.

Aedan: Great! I'm so glad!

Musterprüfung 1, Teil A: *Listening comprehension* ▶ p. 58

Part 1: *Short conversations*
a) B · b) C · c) A · d) A · e) A

Part 2: *Top of the Rock*
a) Central Park
b) 8 am
c) $34 / 34 dollars
d) visit twice in a day / two times
e) wear warm clothes

Part 3: *Concorde – a very special plane*
a) A · b) B · c) C · d) C · e) B

Part 4: *Places in Shakespeare's life*
a) C · b) G · c) E · d) D · e) A

Musterprüfung 1, Teil B: *Text-based tasks* ▶ p. 61

Part 1: *Understanding signs*
a) C · b) A · c) B · d) A · e) C

Part 2: *My favourite British planes*
1) lines 1–14: c)
2) lines 15–20: e)
3) lines 21–27: a)
4) lines 29–40: b)
5) lines 41–49: d)

Part 3: *My favourite British planes*
a) false · b) true · c) not in the text · d) false · e) false

Part 4: *My favourite British planes*
1) C · 2) A · 3) B · 4) A · 5) C

Part 5: *My favourite British planes*

a) However, what had been its big advantage in the 1930s became its big disadvantage ten years later.

b) And that meant the end for the flying boats.

c) It is an interesting period in aviation history that we should never forget.

d) What people most remember about the *Comet* today is that it had a number of crashes which nobody could explain.

e) … and the number of planes built was disappointingly small.

Musterprüfung 1, Teil C: *Use of language* ▶ p. 65

Part 1: *A presentation about Wales*
a) sheep · b) built · c) isn't · d) biggest · e) has · f) many

Part 2: *A presentation about Wales*
a) beautiful (line 8) · b) king (line 9)

Part 3: *A presentation about Wales*
a) region (line 3) · b) taken out of (line 16)

Part 4: *A presentation about Wales*
Lösungsbeispiel:

a) a place that is larger than a village and smaller than a city / a place where people live and work with houses, shops etc. / a place with many streets and buildings / …

b) the opposite of north / one of the four directions: north, east, west and south / the south of a country is the part that is closest to Antarctica / the direction of the sun when it is at its highest point / …

c) to go somewhere else to live / to leave a place to live somewhere else / to go to live in another area or country / to stop living in one place and go to live in another / …

Part 5: *A presentation about Wales*
Lösungsbeispiel:

What is the name of the biggest mountain in Wales? / How do people earn their money today? / What castles can you visit? / How many people live in Wales? / What is the capital of Wales?

Musterprüfung 1, Teil D: *Writing* ▶ p. 66

Part 1
Lösungsbeispiel:

Dear Carly

how are you? I wish you a very happy birthday!

How are you spending your special day? Are you going to have a party with your friends?

I have a present for you – I made a playlist with some of your favourite songs. I'm going to send you the link later.

My own birthday is in June. I'm really excited because we'll be on holiday in Turkey then.

Lots of love
Selin

(74 Wörter)

Part 2
Lösungsbeispiel:

Yesterday was a terrible day. Everything went wrong.
We wanted to surprise our friend Emma with a birthday party
after school. But on my way to school something bad happened:
The cake I was carrying got wet because it started raining. Then
we asked Emma about her plans after school and she told us
that she did not feel well and just wanted to go home.
So unfortunately, the surprise party did not happen. Well, we
didn't have a cake anyway.

(81 Wörter)

Musterprüfung 2, Teil A: *Listening comprehension* ▶ p. 67

Part 1: *Short conversations*
a) C · b) A · c) B · d) C · e) B

Part 2: *Another tourist attraction in Brighton*
a) dirty water
b) 1860
c) safer and healthier
d) £6 / six pounds
e) children younger than 11

Part 3: *Cricket in India*
a) C · b) B · c) A · d) A · e) C

Part 4: *St. Kilda*
a) G · b) A · c) D · d) B · e) F

Musterprüfung 2, Teil B: *Text-based tasks* ▶ p. 70

Part 1: *Understanding signs*
a) B · b) C · c) A · d) A · e) C

Part 2: *The Mousetrap*
1) lines 1–9: c)
2) lines 10–15: e)
3) lines 16–22: a)
4) lines 23–32: b)
5) lines 33–46: d)

Part 3: *The Mousetrap*
a) true · b) not in the text · c) false · d) false · e) true

Part 4: *The Mousetrap*
1) C · 2) A · 3) B · 4) C · 5) A

Part 5: *The Mousetrap*

a) ... making it the longest-running play in the world.

b) ... if you try to book, you may well find that you can't, because
tickets have already sold out.

c) ... the theatre critics in many newspapers were not
impressed.

d) But at the end of every show, the members of the audience
are asked not to reveal the secret or to share it on social
media.

e) And the impressive thing is that, by and large, the secret has
been kept.

Musterprüfung 2, Teil C: *Use of language* ▶ p. 74

Part 1: *The Royal Pavilion in Brighton*
a) standing · b) like · c) too · d) where · e) makes ·
f) entrance

Part 2: *The Royal Pavilion in Brighton*
a) son (line 9) · b) expensive (line 13)

Part 3: *The Royal Pavilion in Brighton*
a) escape (line 16) · b) contrast (line 22)

Part 4: *The Royal Pavilion in Brighton*
Lösungsbeispiel:

a) not normal / different / unusual / the opposite of usual / ...

b) to like something more than another thing / to like
something better than another thing

c) It's the room in the house where you prepare food / room for
cooking / ..

Part 5: *The Royal Pavilion in Brighton*
Lösungsbeispiel:

What colour is the palace? / How many rooms are there in
total? / How many visitors are there every year? / Where in
Brighton is the Royal Pavilion?

Musterprüfung 2, Teil D: *Writing* ▶ p. 75

Part 1
Lösungsbeispiel:

Dear Sir or Madam

I would like to work as a volunteer at one of your summer
camps, but I have a few questions: Do you have a summer camp
in August? I finish school in July and could work all August. Do
you offer accommodation for your volunteers? And what activities do you do with the kids? I work as a soccer coach in my free
time, so I could play soccer with the kids.

I look forward to your reply.

Yours faithfully

(84 Wörter)

Part 2
Lösungsbeispiel:

My favourite app is called *Food Navi*. With this app restaurants
and shops can offer food that they don't use anymore. And
people like you and me can pick it up for little money. *Food Navi*
is amazing because it helps save a lot of good food – and it helps
save money. A disadvantage is that not all shops take part in the
project. So I hope the idea will get more well-known and many
more restaurants and shops will decide to give away their food
instead of throwing it away.

(91 Wörter)

Die Tonaufnahmen (MP3-Dateien) und die Hörtexte findest du online unter www.scook.de.
Deinen persönlichen Zugangscode findest du auf Seite 1 deines Abschlussprüfungstrainers.

Track	Kapitel	Titel	Seite
1	Training Section	Short conversations	7
2	Training Section	A visit to Krakow	7
3	Training Section	A tourist attraction in Brighton	8
4	Training Section	Skyways in the US and Canada	9
5	Training Section	The Niagara Falls (Part 1, Version 1)	10
6	Training Section	The Niagara Falls (Part 1, Version 2)	11
7	Training Section	The Niagara Falls (Part 2, Version 1)	11
8	Training Section	The Niagara Falls (Part 2, Version 2)	12
9	Training Section	The Niagara Falls (Part 3, Version 1)	12
10	Training Section	The Niagara Falls (Part 3, Version 2)	13
11	Training Section	Two fantastic cycle races	13
12	Training Section	Bob Marley	14
13	Musterprüfung 1	Short conversations	58
14	Musterprüfung 1	Top of the Rock	59
15	Musterprüfung 1	Concorde – a very special plane	59
16	Musterprüfung 1	Places in Shakespeare's life	60
17	Musterprüfung 2	Short conversations	67
18	Musterprüfung 2	Another tourist attraction in Brighton	68
19	Musterprüfung 2	Cricket in India	68
20	Musterprüfung 2	St. Kilda	69

Studio: Clarity Studio Berlin
Regie und Aufnahmeleitung: Christian Schmitz
Tontechnik: Hüseyin Dönertaş, Christian Marx, Christian Schmitz

Schritt 5: Überprüfe jetzt deinen Text. Dafür kannst du diese Checklisten verwenden.

Prüfe, ob du die Aufgabenstellung erfüllt hast:	
Hast du eine passende Anrede geschrieben?	☐
Hast du mindestens drei Inhaltspunkte berücksichtigt?	☐
Hast du eine klare Struktur mit Absätzen verwendet?	☐
Hast du eine passende Grußformel verwendet?	☐
Hast du mindestens 60 Wörter geschrieben?	☐

Prüfe auch die Sprache:	
Stimmen die Zeitformen der Verben?	☐
Stimmen die Verneinungen?	☐
Hast du Wörter, bei deren Rechtschreibung du unsicher bist, im Wörterbuch überprüft?	☐
Stimmt die Satzstellung (Subjekt – Verb – Objekt)?	☐
Hast du an das -s nach *he/she/it* gedacht?	☐
Hast du an das -s beim Plural gedacht?	☐
Hast du daran gedacht, die Langformen der Verben zu verwenden?	☐
Hast du einige Verbindungswörter benutzt?	☐

Zweite (längere) Schreibaufgabe: Erlebnisse, Erfahrungen, Meinungen, Vorlieben

Bei der zweiten Schreibaufgabe sollst du über Erlebnisse oder Erfahrungen berichten oder deine Meinung oder Vorlieben zu einem Alltagsthema äußern. Dabei sollst du ungefähr 80 Wörter schreiben. Du erhältst einige Fragestellungen, Ideen oder Redemittel als Hilfsmittel.

1. Über Erfahrungen oder Erlebnisse schreiben

Die Prüfungsaufgabe könnte so aussehen:

Write about a great trip. The following ideas can help you.

| Where? | When? | Who? | Why was it special? |

idea box

camping / hostel / mountains / seaside / city / railway station / airport / train (station) / ferry / weather / adventure / feeling / sights / amazing / climb / hike / ride / …

Write about 80 words.

Schritt 1: Lies das Lösungsbeispiel und bearbeite folgende Aufgaben:

a)   Inhalt:

In einem Erlebnisbericht sollten die wichtigsten *wh*-Fragen beantwortet sein, auch wenn sie nicht in der Aufgabenstellung stehen. Wie sieht es hier aus?

Fragen aus der Aufgabenstellung:

Where: mountains, Black Forest

When: _____

Who: _____

Why special: _____

_____

weitere Fragen:

What: _____

How: _____

Last autumn I went on a great hiking trip in the Black Forest with my cousin Charlie.

The weather was awful, but the trip was still great fun. We hiked along a muddy valley, we climbed steep hills and in the evening we cooked on an open fire. The night in the wet tent wasn't great, but the next day the sun came out. It was an amazing feeling to stand on Feldberg, the highest mountain in the Black Forest. Usually I'm not a sporty person, so I'm really proud that I didn't give up. Charlie and I talked and laughed a lot and met really nice people who helped us start the fire in the rain.

I think I'll organize a longer hiking trip for next year, and I hope we will be luckier with the weather!

Tipp

Du musst die Fragen, Ideen und Wörter in der Aufgabe nicht unbedingt benutzen, um die volle Punktzahl zu erhalten. Sie helfen dir aber, deinen Text zu gliedern und zu gestalten.

b) Sprache:

1. Über Erlebnisse berichtet man in der Vergangenheit. Notiere alle Verben im *simple past:*

    <hr/>

    <hr/>

> **Tipp**
>
> Eine gute Vorbereitung für die zweite Schreibaufgabe ist es, das *simple past* zu wiederholen. Nutze dazu z. B. die interaktiven Übungen auf www.scook.de.

    Welche anderen Zeitformen kommen vor?

    *   *simple present* (andauernde Zustände): _____

    *   *will-future* (Pläne): _____

2. Adjektive machen den Erlebnisbericht lebendiger. Notiere die Adjektive:

    <hr/>

    <hr/>

> **Tipp**
>
> Behalte stets deine Wörterzahl im Blick. Wenn dein Text zu kurz ist, kannst du noch passende Adjektive oder Verbindungswörter einfügen.

3. Verbindungswörter *(linking words)* und Zeitwörter *(time words)* strukturieren den Text. Notiere

    sie: _____

Schritt 2: Jetzt bist du dran! Berichte von einem ganz besonderen Ausflug oder einer tollen Reise, die du gemacht hast. Orientiere dich an den Pluspunkten im Lösungsbeispiel *(wh*-Fragen, Zeitformen, Adjektive, Verbindungswörter).

> **Tipp**
>
> Wenn dir kein eigenes Erlebnis einfällt, kannst du natürlich auch eins erfinden!

Schritt 3: Überprüfe jetzt deinen Text. Dafür kannst du diese Checklisten verwenden.

Prüfe, ob du die Aufgabenstellung erfüllt hast:	
Berichtest du über ein positives Reiseerlebnis?	☐
Beantwortet dein Text einige wichtige *wh*-Fragen?	☐
Hast du ungefähr 80 Wörter geschrieben?	☐

Prüfe auch die Sprache:	
Erzählst du von deinem Erlebnis im *simple past*?	☐
Enthält dein Bericht einige Adjektive?	☐
Hast du deinen Text durch Verbindungswörter *(but, because, so, although ...)* strukturiert?	☐
Hast du Wörter, bei deren Rechtschreibung du unsicher bist, im Wörterbuch überprüft?	☐
Stimmt die Satzstellung (Subjekt – Verb – Objekt)?	☐
Hast du an das -*s* nach *he/she/it* gedacht?	☐
Hast du an das -*s* beim Plural gedacht?	☐

2. Über Vorlieben schreiben, seine Meinung äußern

Die Prüfungsaufgabe könnte auch so aussehen:

> Write about your favourite TV programme. The following ideas can help you.
>
> | Type? | When? | Who with? | Why? |
> |---|---|---|---|
>
> **idea box**
>
> sports show / cartoons / music show / reality show / crime series / comedy / soaps / exciting / entertaining / relaxing / interesting / feeling / watch with / ...
>
> Write about 80 words.

Schritt 1: Die Fragen aus der Aufgabenstellung bieten eine gute Orientierung – du kannst sie um weitere *wh*-Fragen ergänzen. Entscheide dich für eine Lieblingssendung und mache dir Notizen:

	Beispiel:	Meine Notizen:
name	*Tatort*	
type	*crime series*	
what	*different police teams solve crimes*	
who with	*with my family*	
when	*in the evening*	
where	*living room, at home*	
why	*exciting, relaxing, Cologne*	

Schritt 2: Schreibe nun deinen Text. Folge dabei den Punkten aus deinen Notizen und verbinde sie mit geeigneten Verbindungswörtern.

Aber Achtung! Hier geht es nicht um die Vergangenheit, sondern um aktuelle Vorlieben und eine aktuelle Sendung. Daher schreibst du deinen Text überwiegend im *simple present*.

> **Tipp**
>
> Auch hier gilt: Wenn dir die Frage nach deiner Lieblingssendung zu persönlich ist oder du keine Lieblingssendung hast, schreibst du einfach über eine andere Sendung.

Schritt 3: Überprüfe jetzt deinen Text. Dafür kannst du diese Checklisten verwenden.

Prüfe, ob du die Aufgabenstellung erfüllt hast:	
Schreibst du über eine Fernsehsendung, die du gerne magst?	☐
Beantwortet dein Text einige wichtige *wh*-Fragen?	☐
Hast du ungefähr 80 Wörter geschrieben?	☐

Prüfe auch die Sprache:	
Beschreibst du deine TV-Vorlieben im *simple present*?	☐
Hast du deinen Text durch Verbindungswörter *(but, because, so, although ...)* strukturiert?	☐
Hast du Wörter, bei deren Rechtschreibung du unsicher bist, im Wörterbuch überprüft?	☐
Stimmt die Satzstellung (Subjekt – Verb – Objekt)?	☐
Hast du an das -*s* nach *he/she/it* gedacht?	☐
Hast du an das -*s* beim Plural gedacht?	☐

Die Kommunikationsprüfung

Die Kommunikationsprüfung ist ein wichtiger Teil der Hauptschulabschlussprüfung. Sie findet meist im zweiten Schulhalbjahr an deiner Schule statt. Geprüft wirst du durch deinen Englischlehrer bzw. deine Englischlehrerin und eine weitere Fachkraft deiner Schule.

1. Ablauf und Bewertung

Bei der Kommunikationsprüfung werden in der Regel zwei Schüler oder Schülerinnen zusammen geprüft. In Ausnahmefällen kann es aber auch passieren, dass du allein geprüft wirst, z. B. bei einer ungeraden Klassenstärke. Pro Prüfling stehen ca. 15 Minuten Zeit zur Verfügung, die gleichmäßig auf die drei Prüfungsteile verteilt werden. Eine Vorbereitungszeit gibt es nicht. Insgesamt kannst du bei der Kommunikationsprüfung 30 Punkte erreichen – so viel wie bei keinem anderen Prüfungsteil.

Punkte erhältst du nicht nur für deine sprachlichen Fähigkeiten (Wortschatz, Grammatik, Verständlichkeit), sondern auch dafür, dass du auf deinen Gesprächspartner eingehst, auf das Gesagte reagierst und dazu beiträgst, das Gespräch am Laufen zu halten.

Teil 1: Monologisches Sprechen: Präsentation (10 Punkte)

Hier sollst du zeigen, dass du ein Thema selbstständig erarbeiten und mithilfe passender Medien verständlich darstellen kannst. Das Thema stimmst du vorher mit deiner Englischlehrerin oder deinem Englischlehrer ab. Am Ende kann es sein, dass dir noch Fragen zu deinem Thema gestellt werden. Ihr könnt auch zu zweit ein Thema vorbereiten und euch den Vortrag dann aufteilen.

Teil 2: Dialogisches Sprechen: Sich über ein vorgegebenes Thema austauschen (10 Punkte)

Ihr erhaltet beide eine Rollenkarte *(prompt card)*, auf der das Thema und eine Situation vorgegeben sind. Die eine Karte enthält Fragen zum Thema, die andere Antworten. Ihr sollt euch nun im Gespräch über das Thema austauschen. Nach der Hälfte der Zeit erhaltet ihr neue Karten zu einem weiteren Thema. Wenn du vorher die Karte mit den Fragen hattest, bekommst du nun die Karte mit den Antworten und umgekehrt.

> **Tipp**
>
> Solltest du etwas nicht verstehen, zögere nicht, auf Englisch nachzufragen:
>
> *Sorry, I didn't understand what you said.*
>
> *Sorry, could you repeat that, please?*
>
> Es ist wichtig, dass du alle Fragen richtig verstehst und dass keine zu langen Gesprächspausen entstehen.

Teil 3: Sprachmittlung: Deutsch – Englisch, Englisch - Deutsch (10 Punkte)

Euch wird eine Situation zwischen einer deutschsprachigen und einer englischsprachigen Person vorgegeben, in der ihr vermitteln sollt. Die eine Rolle übernimmt deine Lehrerin oder dein Lehrer, die andere Rolle der andere Prüfling – jeweils mithilfe einer Sprechkarte. Deine Aufgabe besteht darin, die deutschsprachigen Inhalte auf Englisch und die englischsprachigen Inhalte auf Deutsch wiederzugeben. Dabei geht es nicht um eine wörtliche Übersetzung, sondern um eine sinngemäße Übertragung.

2. Aufgabenformate in Baden-Württemberg

In diesem Kapitel lernst du die typischen Aufgabenformate kennen, die dich bei der Kommunikationsprüfung erwarten. Da es sich in der Regel um eine Tandemprüfung handelt, ist es sinnvoll, dich zusammen mit einem Freund oder einer Freundin vorzubereiten. Die Tipp-Kästen enthalten nützliche Strategien.

Teil 1: Monologisches Sprechen

Auf den ersten Teil der Prüfung kannst du dich am besten vorbereiten. Es lohnt sich also, deinen Vortrag gut zu planen und einzuüben!

Schritt 1: Du wählst ein Thema aus, mit dem du dich auskennst, und besprichst es mit deiner Lehrkraft. Du könntest zum Beispiel über deine Familie, ein Hobby, eine Reise, deine Lieblingsband, dein Lieblingstier oder deinen Sport sprechen.

> **Tipp**
>
> In diesem Teil der Prüfung geht es um dich und deine Themen. Du sollst zeigen, dass du dein Thema verständlich darstellen und zusammenhängend darüber sprechen kannst. Fachwissen ist hier nicht gefragt.

Schritt 2: Du sammelst Ideen, z. B. mithilfe von Karteikarten oder in einer Mindmap:

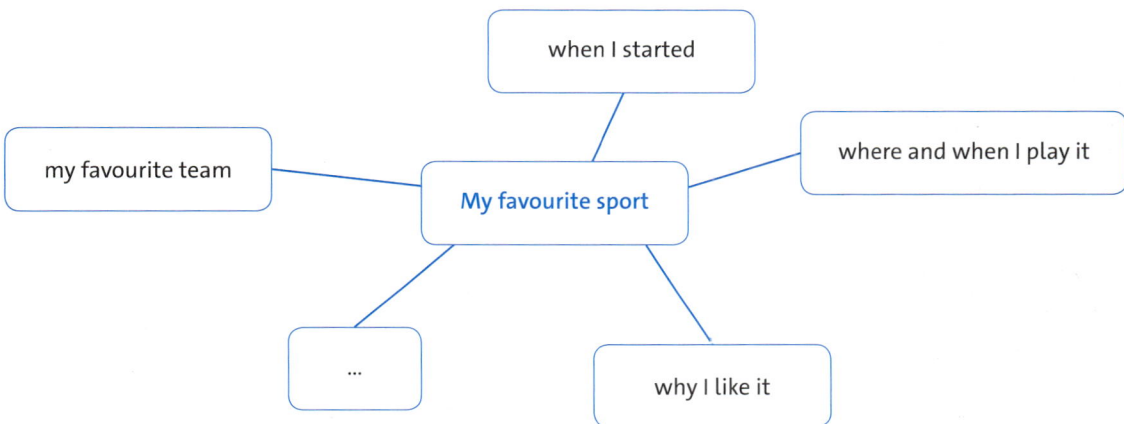

Überlege auch frühzeitig, welche Medien du einsetzen möchtest: Suche nach geeigneten Fotos (z. B. von deiner Familie oder deinem Fußballverein) oder Gegenständen (z. B. Urlaubssouvenirs oder etwas, das du sammelst). Du könntest auch ein Plakat oder eine kurze Computer-Präsentation vorbereiten.

Schritt 3: Du ordnest deine Ideen:

- Womit fängst du an?
- Welche Reihenfolge ist am besten?
- Womit hörst du auf?

> **Tipp**
>
> Notiere deine Ideen stichwortartig auf Karteikarten – für jede Idee eine Karte. Nun kannst du verschiedene Reihenfolgen ausprobieren.

Schritt 4: Du arbeitest deinen Vortrag aus. Dafür gibt es viele nützliche und typische Redewendungen. Ergänze eigene Ideen in der Tabelle.

Tipp

Überprüfe die Aussprache der Wörter in einem Wörterbuch oder frage deine Lehrerin oder deinen Lehrer.

My presentation		
Einleitung	I'd like to tell you about my ...	
	Today I'm going to talk about ...	
	Last summer I went on a trip to ... with ...	
Mittelteil	First I'd like to tell you ... / I'll start with ...	
	Then I'll look at ... / Then I'll talk about ...	
	Next ... And finally ...	
	For example, ... / To give you an example: ...	
	I'd like to show you ...	
	This picture shows ...	
	Let's have a look at ...	
	Look at this stamp/photo/postcard/...	
Schluss	That's the end of my talk.	
	Thank you for listening.	
	Do you have any questions?	

Schritt 5: Übe deinen Vortrag ein. Wenn du dich einiger-maßen sicher fühlst, halte deinen Vortrag frei vor einem Spiegel, einer Freundin oder einem Freund oder deinen Eltern. Du kannst dich auch mit dem Smartphone filmen. Achte auf Folgendes:

- Versuche, flüssig zu sprechen, und verzichte auf „ähs".
- Sprich langsam und deutlich.
- Schaue deine Zuhörer immer mal wieder an.

Tipp

Du darfst Stichworte als Gedankenstütze mit in die Prüfung nehmen. Das gibt dir Sicherheit. Du solltest aber auf keinen Fall an ihnen „kleben".

Tipp

Stopp die Zeit, die du für deinen Vortrag brauchst. Sind es mehr als fünf Minuten, solltest du überlegen, welche Idee du weglässt. Sind es weniger als fünf Minuten, solltest du nach weiteren Ideen suchen.

Schritt 6: Bewerte dich selbst oder lass dich bewerten (☺ / ☺ / ☹). Dafür kannst du diese Checklisten verwenden.

Inhalt und Darstellung:	
Du hast das Thema umfassend dargestellt und viele Informationen gegeben.	
Dein Vortrag war gut strukturiert (Einleitung, Mittelteil, Schluss).	
Du hast passende und anschauliche Medien gezeigt.	
Du hattest Blickkontakt zu deinem Publikum.	
Du konntest auf Rückfragen Antwort geben.	

Sprache:	
Du hast flüssig und verständlich gesprochen.	
Du hast weitgehend frei gesprochen.	
Deine Aussprache war weitgehend korrekt.	
Du hast kaum oder nur wenige Fehler (Wortschatz, Grammatik) gemacht.	
Du hast einige typische Redewendungen benutzt.	

Teil 2: Dialogisches Sprechen

Beim zweiten Teil der Prüfung führst du mit dem anderen Prüfling einen Dialog. Ihr erhaltet dafür jeweils eine Rollenkarte zu einem bestimmten Thema – ein Prüfling mit Informationen zu dem Thema, der/die andere mit Fragen:

Karate club	A

**You are interested in your school's karate club.
Find out some details. Ask at least 5 questions.**

- who?
- when?
- where?
- costs?
- clothes?
- further information?

Karate club · B

**You are a member of your school's karate club.
Please give some information about it.**

Are you 12 years or older? Then join our karate club!

All levels welcome!

- Monday and Wednesday 3–5 o'clock
- at the gym
- For free ☺!
- Just bring comfortable clothes.

Further information:
Kevin: 0162 208 36 40 (karate-kevin@example.net)

Schritt 1: Suche dir einen Partner oder eine Partnerin. Seht euch zunächst beide Karten an (A und B). Versucht dann, aus den Stichwörtern auf Karte A die Fragen zu entwickeln. Dabei gibt es oft mehrere Lösungen! Ergänzt weitere Fragen in der Tabelle.

Tipp
Wiederhole das Bilden von Fragen mit und ohne Fragewort. Nutze dazu z. B. die interaktiven Übungen auf www.scook.de.

Schritt 2: Überlegt euch nun auch gemeinsam die Antworten. Wichtig ist dabei, dass ihr nicht zu einsilbig antwortet oder einfach nur von der Karte ablest, sondern ganze Sätze bildet. Auch für die Antwort gibt es verschiedene Möglichkeiten. Ergänzt die Vorschläge in der Tabelle.

Tipp
Oft geht es hier um das Datum oder Uhrzeiten, um Telefonnummern und E-Mail-Adressen, um Adressen oder um Preisangaben. Diese Dinge kannst du vor der Prüfung gut üben! Nutze dafür auch die Kästen auf S. 56.

	Frage	Antwort
who?	Who can come to the karate club? Who can take part? Who is the club for?	Everybody over 12 can come. All levels are welcome. Beginners can take part too.
when?	When does the club meet? When does it take place? What are the practice times?	The club meets on … at …
where?	Where does the club meet? Where do you practise? _____?	

	Frage	Antwort
costs?	How much does it cost? How much do I have to pay? _____ ?	
clothes?	What do I have to wear? _____ ? _____ ?	
information?	Where can I get further information? _____ ? _____ ?	

Schritt 3: Führt nun den Dialog zweimal: jeder einmal in jeder Rolle (A/B). Es macht auf die Prüfer einen guten Eindruck, wenn sich euer Gespräch möglichst natürlich anhört. Zum Beispiel solltet ihr höflich zueinander sein, euch begrüßen, euch bedanken, euch verabschieden:

> **Tipp**
> Es ist wichtig, dass ihr aufeinander reagiert, wie man es auch im echten Leben täte. So sollte man die Antworten, die man erhält, zur Kenntnis nehmen, ehe man die nächste Frage stellt, z. B.:
>
> A: *How much does it cost?*
>
> B: *Nothing. It's free!*
>
> A: *That's cool! And what do I have to wear?*

Hi Carla. I'm interested in the karate club. Can I ask you some questions?

Hi Cem. Sure! What would you like to know?

Can you tell me where ...? Do you know when...? And how much ...?

Yes! The club meets ... And you can ...

That sounds great. Thanks!

You're welcome!

> **Tipp**
> Ihr solltet bei diesem Dialog nicht mit dem Prüfer oder der Prüferin reden, sondern miteinander. Schaut euch also dabei an!

Schritt 4: Jetzt bist du dran – diesmal (wie in der Prüfung!) ohne Vorbereitung. Such dir dazu einen Partner oder eine Partnerin. Ideal ist es, wenn noch eine dritte Person dabei ist, die euch anschließend Feedback gibt. In der Regel beginnt die Person, die die Rollenkarte mit den Fragen hat.

An online advert	A

You want to buy a used bike and found an online advert. You call the seller to find out more about the bike. Ask at least 5 questions.

- how old?
- sell why?
- size?
- lights OK?
- price?
- pick up where/when?

An online advert	B

You want to sell your old bike and advertised it online. Somebody saw your advert and calls you. Please give more information.

- only two years old
- already too small
- wheel size: 28 inches
- lights aren't working
- price: £ 125
- address: 34 Benny Lane, Practice Town
- best time: Wednesday, 6 pm

Tipp

Denkt daran: Wenn man eine fremde Person anruft, stellt man sich vor und sagt, worum es geht.

Tipp

Frage nach, wenn du etwas nicht verstanden hast:

Could you say that again, please?

Sorry, what did you say?

Schritt 5: Bewertet nun euren Partner oder eure Partnerin oder lasst euch Feedback von der dritten Person geben (☺ / ☺ / ☹).

Dafür könnt ihr diese Checklisten verwenden.

Situation und Reaktion:	
Du hast dich schnell auf die Situation auf deiner Rollenkarte eingelassen.	☐
Du hast das Gespräch mitgestaltet, Initiative ergriffen, das Gespräch mit aufrechterhalten.	☐
Du bist auf deinen Partner oder deine Partnerin eingegangen, hast angemessen reagiert.	☐
Du hast dich an allgemeine Gesprächsregeln gehalten (Begrüßung, Höflichkeit etc.).	☐
Du hast in ganzen Sätzen gesprochen.	☐
Du hattest Blickkontakt zu deinem Partner oder deiner Partnerin.	☐

Sprache:	
Du hast flüssig und verständlich gesprochen.	☐
Du hast einen breiten Wortschatz verwendet.	☐
Deine Aussprache war weitgehend korrekt.	☐
Du hast kaum oder nur wenige Fehler (Wortschatz, Grammatik) gemacht.	☐
Du hast einige typische Redewendungen benutzt.	☐

Teil 3: Sprachmittlung

Beim dritten und letzten Teil der Kommunikationsprüfung wird dir eine Situation vorgegeben, in der du die Rolle des Dolmetschers zwischen einer englischsprachigen und einer deutschsprachigen Person übernimmst. Diese Rollen werden von dem anderen Prüfling und deinem Lehrer oder deiner Lehrerin übernommen und du musst spontan zwischen beiden vermitteln:

Tipp

Wenn du ein Wort nicht kennst, sage es anders:

| Selbstbedienung | → *There's no waiter.* |
| Betriebsfahrt | → *This is the wrong bus.* |

Wenn dir das Gegenteil einfällt, kannst du es verneinen:

Es ist sehr <u>ruhig</u> hier. → *It <u>isn't noisy</u> at all.*

At the football club

You're at the football club and meet Adelola, a girl from Nigeria. She would like to join the club and has some questions. But Adelola doesn't speak German and the coach doesn't speak English. Can you help them?

Adelola (teacher)	Mediation (you)	Coach (student)
I'd like to know if boys and girls play together in mixed teams.		
	Das Mädchen …	
		Zurzeit gibt es leider keine gemischten Mannschaften.
OK. But do you have a girls' team?		
		Ja, wir haben eine Mannschaft für Mädchen zwischen 12 und 16 Jahren.
That's great! And what are the practice times?		
		Die Mädchenmannschaft trainiert freitags um 16 Uhr. Sie kann gerne nächste Woche kommen.
I will. Thank you so much!		

Schritt 1: Lies dir einmal das gesamte Dialoggerüst durch. Mache dir klar, wann du auf Englisch und wann du auf Deutsch sprechen musst. Löse dann die Aufgabe mithilfe der Tipps einmal schriftlich – zur Übung. In der Prüfung hast du keine Vorbereitungszeit!

> **Tipp**
>
> Achtung, Perspektivwechsel!
>
> | | |
> |---|---|
> | Adelola sagt: | *I'd like to know …* |
> | Du sagst: | Das Mädchen (oder: sie) möchte wissen … |
>
> oder:
>
> | | |
> |---|---|
> | Der Trainer sagt: | Sie kann gerne nächste Woche kommen. |
> | Du sagst: | *You can …* |

Schritt 2: Such dir zwei Partner, die die Rollen von Adelola und dem Trainer übernehmen. Macht nun zwei mündliche Durchgänge – einmal mit deinen Notizen aus Schritt 1, einmal ohne.

> **Tipp**
>
> Sprachmittlung ist keine wörtliche Übersetzung. Du musst nur das Wesentliche wiedergeben. Unwichtige Details, Füllwörter oder Ausrufe kannst du ruhig weglassen.
>
> | | |
> |---|---|
> | Adelola sagt: | *That's great! And what are the practice times?* |
> | Du sagst: | (Super!) Und wann …? |
>
> Oder:
>
> | | |
> |---|---|
> | Der Trainer sagt: | Zur Zeit gibt es leider keine gemischten Mannschaften. |
> | Du sagst: | (Unfortunately) there are … |

Schritt 3: Brauchst du noch Übung mit dem Perspektivwechsel (Wechsel der Pronomen)? Stell dir vor, du bist mit deinem Vater im Ausland beim Arzt, und fülle diese Tabelle aus:

Dein Vater sagt …	… und so gibst du das an die Ärztin weiter:
Sag der Ärztin bitte, dass **ich** Kopfschmerzen habe.	*He has a headache.*
Und **ich** habe Halsschmerzen.	_____ *a sore throat.*
Können **Sie mir** helfen? Kann **sie mir** helfen?	*Can _____ help _____?*
Kann **ich** mit Kreditkarte zahlen?	_____ *by credit card?*
Ich habe leider kein Bargeld.	_____ *any cash.*

Die Ärztin sagt …	… und so gibst du das an deinen Vater weiter:
I can give **him/you** headache pills.	*Sie kann dir Kopfschmerztabletten geben.*
He/You should drink a lot.	
Sorry, **we** don't take credit cards.	
I can show **you** the way to a cash machine.	
Call **me** if you're still sick next week.	

Schritt 4: Jetzt bist du dran! Nun übst du mit einer neuen Aufgabe – diesmal (wie in der Prüfung!) ohne Vorbereitung. Um die Prüfungssituation am besten nachzuahmen, suchst du dir zwei Partner und stellst eine Stoppuhr auf fünf Minuten.

At the lost and found
Aedan from Ireland is visiting you. He lost his phone at the station, so you go to the lost and found office with him. But Aedan doesn't speak German and the assistant doesn't speak English. Can you help them?

Aedan (teacher)	Mediation (you)	Assistant (student)
I lost my phone. Can you help me?		
	Er …	
		Ich brauche da mehr Details. Wann und wo hat er es verloren?
I think it was at the smoothie stand, at around 6 pm.		
		Und wie sieht es aus?
It's a white Sumsang BX7. And it has stickers on the back.		
		Er hat Glück. Das Handy ist hier. Ich gehe es holen.
Great! I'm so glad!		

Tipp

Duzen und Siezen

Wenn du aus dem Deutschen ins Englische vermittelst, kannst du die Frage Duzen oder Siezen ignorieren, denn im Englischen ist es immer *you(r)*.

Beispiel:　Können Sie bar zahlen? ⟶
　　　　　　Kannst du bar zahlen? ⟶ *Can you pay cash?*

Wenn du aber aus dem Englischen ins Deutsche vermittelst, musst du überlegen, wie du das englische *you(r)* wiedergibst. Redest du mit einer Person, die du eher duzen oder eher siezen würdest?

Beispiel:　*You should drink a lot.* ⟶ Sie sollten viel trinken. (zu fremden Erwachsenen)
　　　　　　　　　　　　　　　　⟶ Du solltest viel trinken. (zu jungen Leuten, Bekannten, deinen Eltern ...)

Schritt 5: Bitte deine Partner, dich zu bewerten. Dafür könnt ihr diese Checkliste verwenden.

Sprachmittlung:	
Du hast die wesentlichen Informationen vollständig und sinngemäß wiedergegeben.	☐
Du hast, wenn nötig, die Perspektive (das Pronomen) gewechselt.	☐
Du hast landestypische Besonderheiten (z. B. *am/pm* bei Uhrzeiten) angemessen wiedergegeben.	☐
Du hast einen breiten und passenden Wortschatz verwendet.	☐
Du hast Wörter, die dir nicht einfielen, angemessen ersetzt oder umschrieben.	☐
Du hast kaum oder nur wenige Fehler (Grammatik, Wortschatz) gemacht.	☐
Du hast weitgehend flüssig und verständlich gesprochen.	☐

3. Nützliches für die Kommunikationsprüfung

Phone numbers:

Bei Telefonnummern sagt man *oh* für die Null:

0162 208 36 40 = oh-one-six-two, two-oh-eight, three-six, four-oh

Email addresses:

karate-kevin@example.net:

karate-dash-kevin-at-example-dot-net

The date:

Wiederhole die Monate und Wochentage! Beachte:

Man schreibt:	Man sagt:
1st March	the first of March
2nd May	the second of May
3rd June	the third of June
4th August	the fourth of August
5th October	the fifth of October
21st December	the twenty-first of December

The time:

8.00	eight o'clock
8.10	ten past eight
8.15	a quarter past eight
8.30	half past eight
8.40	twenty to nine
8.45	a quarter to nine
am	morgens/vormittags
pm	nachmittags/abends

British money:

Man schreibt:	Man sagt:
50 p	fifty p (pence)
£ 0.50	fifty p (pence)
£ 2.00	two pounds
£ 3.50	three pounds fifty
£ 3.99	three pounds ninety-nine

The alphabet:

a	ay	n	en
b	bee	o	oh
c	cee	p	pea
d	dee	q	queue
e	ee	r	are
f	ef	s	es
g	gee	t	tea
h	eytch	u	you
i	eye	v	vee
j	jay	w	double-you
k	kay	x	ex
l	el	y	why
m	em	z	zed

großes A/B/C/... = *capital* A/B/C/...

ABSCHLUSS-
PRÜFUNGS-
TRAINER

Hauptschulabschluss
Baden-Württemberg

Musterprüfungen

Musterprüfung 1

A – Listening comprehension   20 pts

Part 1: Short conversations   ____ / 5

🎧
13

You will hear five short conversations. You will hear each conversation twice.
There is one question for each conversation.

Mark A, B or C.

a) What did the boy have for breakfast today?

cereals and juice	a warm breakfast	toast with marmalade
A ☐	B ☐	C ☐

b) Why is the girl worried?

Her mum is in hospital.	Her dad is driving too fast.	Her dad isn't wearing a seat belt.
A ☐	B ☐	C ☐

c) Where did Sabrina go last weekend?

town walls	museum	shopping
A ☐	B ☐	C ☐

d) What activity will they probably do at the school fair?

guessing the number of sweets	face painting	shaving balloons
A ☐	B ☐	C ☐

e) Where's the nearest post office?

in Hudson Street	in King Street	in Miller Road
A ☐	B ☐	C ☐

Part 2: Top of the Rock ____/5

🎧 14

You will hear a podcast about a famous sight in New York. You will hear the information twice.

Listen and complete the table.

The Top of the Rock Observation Deck		
	number of floors up:	70
a)	great view of buildings and ...	
b)	opens at:	
c)	price for 16 year olds:	
d)	advantage of Sun&Stars ticket:	visit _____
e)	tip for night visits:	wear _____

Part 3: Concorde – a very special plane ____/5

🎧 15

You will hear a radio programme about *Concorde*, a very special plane. You will hear the information twice.

Mark A, B or C.

a) *Concorde* is special because it was ...

A ☐ the fastest plane ever.

B ☐ the first plane to fly to New York.

C ☐ almost as fast as sound.

b) The *Concorde* passenger service began in ...

A ☐ 1969.

B ☐ 1976.

C ☐ 1996.

c) A big problem for *Concorde* was that ...

A ☐ it was tested too much.

B ☐ it was difficult to build.

C ☐ only two airlines bought it.

d) *Concorde* was taken out of service in ...

A ☐ 1997.

B ☐ 2000.

C ☐ 2003.

e) People didn't want to fly on *Concorde* anymore because ...

A ☐ it was too expensive.

B ☐ there was a terrible crash.

C ☐ Russia built a faster plane.

Part 4: Places in Shakespeare's life ___/ 5

You will hear a presentation about William Shakespeare. You will hear the presentation twice. What were these places in his life?

Write a letter, A-H, next to each place.

a) Henley Street ☐	A	place of death
b) Town hall ☐	B	university
c) London ☐	C	birthplace
d) Globe ☐	D	theatre
e) Stratford ☐	E	place of work
	F	farm
	G	school
	H	pub

B – Text-based tasks   25 pts

Part 1: Understanding signs   ____ / 5

What information do these signs give you? Write down the correct letters.

a)

```
DANGER
HARD HAT
AREA
```

A Hard hats are dangerous for your head.

B You mustn't wear hats here.

C You have to wear a safety helmet.

b)

```
BUILDING SITE
UNAUTHORISED
PERSONS
KEEP OUT
```

A People without permission can't get in.

B Only authors are allowed in.

C This building is illegal.

c)

```
WARNING
HEAVY PLANT AND
MACHINERY
OPERATE ON SITE
```

A There's an electronic alarm system.

B Large machines are used here.

C Carrying heavy plants can hurt your back.

d)

```
ALL VISITORS AND
DRIVERS  MUST
REPORT TO
SITE OFFICE
```

A You have to go to an office to say what you want.

B You can visit the builders in the office.

C You can drive to the office.

e)

```
CCTV WARNING
THIS SITE IS
UNDER 24 HOURS
SURVEILLANCE
```

A This site is closed for a film production.

B A TV reporter has warned about this site.

C There are security cameras at this site.

Part 2 – Part 5: Text

Read the following text carefully and carry out the tasks from parts 2, 3, 4 and 5.

My favourite British planes

Sanjay Gupta, Senior Flight Officer

My favourite British plane is the *Empire* – called the *Short Empire* because it was built by a company called *Short Brothers*. It was perfect for its time, which was in the 1930s. Back then many places in the world didn't have airports, and the amazing thing about the *Empire* was that it landed on lakes or on the sea. It didn't have to have a landing strip – just a big area of water would do. That's why they were so often called flying boats. And you could even say that it kept the British Empire together because it flew and carried mail from London to South Africa, Australia or the Caribbean.

However, what had been its big advantage in the 1930s became its big disadvantage ten years later. Taking off from land became faster and easier, while taking off from water was slower and more difficult. And that meant the end for the flying boats.

A total of 42 *Empires* were built, but unfortunately no *Empire* flying boat exists today. Some of them crashed, others were destroyed during World War II. The last *Empire* flying boat was broken up into pieces and sold in Australia in 1948. It is an interesting period in aviation history that we should never forget.

Carmina Diego, Pilot

I agree that the *Empire* was a great plane, but my vote would be for the *Comet*. It was built after World War II and had its first passenger flight in 1952. What people most remember about the *Comet* today is that it had a number of crashes which nobody could explain. By the time the engineers found out that it was the new technology in the engine that was responsible for the problems, it was too late. The crashes had turned the airlines against the *Comet*, and the number of planes built was disappointingly small.

But in my opinion this is unfair. To begin with, the *Comet* was very successful and passengers loved it. And it was a fantastically modern plane for its time. In fact, what makes it so special in the history of flying is that it was the world's very first passenger jet. The only jet planes back then were military planes, so the *Comet* is the grandad of all our passenger jets today.

Part 2   ___ / 5

Match the letter of the headings with the correct number of the parts of the text.

Write down the correct answers. Example: 6) – f)

1)	lines 1–14	a)	All gone now
2)	lines 15–20	b)	Terrible accidents
3)	lines 21–27	c)	Connecting the world
4)	lines 29–40	d)	Built for travel
5)	lines 41–49	e)	Strength turns into weakness

Part 3   ____ / 5

> Decide whether the statements are 'true', 'false' or 'not in the text'.
>
> Write down the correct answers. Example: f) – not in the text

a) The *Short Empire* got its name because it was very small.

b) When more landing strips were built, the flying boats were no longer needed.

c) No museum wanted to show the old flying boats.

d) Engineers never discovered what was wrong with the *Comet*.

e) Airlines didn't buy the *Comet* because it was unpopular with passengers.

Part 4   ____ / 5

> Complete the sentences by choosing the correct ending according to the text.
>
> Write down the correct answers. Example: 6) – A

1) The *Short Empire* was special because it ...

    A was the first plane ever.

    B could fly to Australia.

    C didn't need an airport.

2) The flying boats transported mostly ...

    A letters.

    B water.

    C soldiers.

3) The *Comet* was special because it ...

    A had a modern engine.

    B carried many passengers.

    C was a military plane.

4) Passengers in the 1950s ...

    A enjoyed flying in a *Comet*.

    B preferred the *Short Empire*.

    C were afraid of accidents.

5) All modern passenger planes are ...

    A modelled on the *Short Empire*.

    B much faster than the *Empire* and the *Comet*.

    C developed from the *Comet*.

Part 5

> Find the corresponding sentence parts or sentences in the text that mean the same and write them down.

a) But in the 1940s the upside of a decade ago turned into a downside.

b) As a consequence, the flying boats had no future.

c) We should always remember this exciting phase in the history of flying.

d) People never forgot the fact that many *Comet* planes had accidents for unknown reasons.

e) Unfortunately, only a few planes were produced.

C – Use of language

15 pts

A presentation about Wales

Most of central Wales is very hilly, and the highest mountains in Wales are higher than any mountain in England. Because the region is so hilly, most of the bigger towns are on the coast. In the centre there are lots of farms and villages, and ______a)______ and cows everywhere. You'll also find lots of beautiful castles in Wales because when an English king wanted to make Wales part of his kingdom, he ______b)______ lots of castles to control the Welsh population. Most of these castles are still standing.

But Wales ______c)______ all fields and castles. The south of Wales was once one of the world's ______d)______ producers of coal: it was taken out of the mines here and shipped as far away as Australia. Lots of industries grew around the coal mines, so the population grew too. The south of Wales still ______e)______ its highest population of all time today – although ______f)______ people have moved away since the coal mines closed. In fact, so many Welsh people have emigrated to Australia that its most-heavily populated state is called New South ... Wales!

Part 1

____ / 6

Read the text and find the correct word. Write down the correct word.

a)	sheep	sheep's	ships
b)	build	built	builds
c)	doesn't	aren't	isn't
d)	most	biggest	least
e)	had	have	has
f)	many	much	lots

Part 2

____ / 2

Find the opposites in the text. Write down the correct answer and the line.

a) ugly

b) queen

Part 3

____ / 2

Find the synonyms in the text. Write down the correct answer and the line.

a) area

b) removed from

Part 4 ____/ 2

> Choose **two** of the following words from the text and give a definition.

a) town (line 5)

b) south (line 19)

c) move away (line 21)

Part 5 ____/ 3

> You want to know more about Wales. Ask **three** questions.

D – Writing 20 pts

Part 1 ____/ 8

> You have a pen friend in Ireland. It's his/her birthday. Write an email.
>
> Include **at least 3** of the following points:
>
> - happy birthday
> - spend the day – how?
> - present(s)
> - your own birthday
>
> Write at least 60 words.

Part 2 ____/ 12

> Write about a terrible day. The following ideas can help you.
>
> | where/when/who? | What happened? | feeling? | Why was it bad? |
>
> **idea box**
>
> accident / storm / get hurt / miss plane, train, ferry, bus … / lose my … / get lost / meet … / die / nervous / scared / embarrassed / angry / sad / …
>
> Write about 80 words.

Musterprüfung 2

A – Listening comprehension   20 pts

Part 1: Short conversations   ____ / 5

> You will hear five short conversations. You will hear each conversation twice.
> There is one question for each conversation.
>
> Mark A, B or C.

17

a) Why is Megan late?

She had an accident.	She crashed into a car door.	She had a problem with her bike.
A ☐	B ☐	C ☐

b) Who does the boy want to visit?

an ex-neighbour	an aunt	a friend in London
A ☐	B ☐	C ☐

c) What were people at the dinner party impressed about?

the women's long dresses	Sebastian's fine clothes	Sebastian's expensive hat
A ☐	B ☐	C ☐

d) What will the weather be like at the weekend?

rainy and windy	wet and grey	cloudy and dry
A ☐	B ☐	C ☐

e) Where does the boy want to put his clothes?

in a bookcase	on a shelf	in a wardrobe
A ☐	B ☐	C ☐

Part 2: Another tourist attraction in Brighton ____ / 5

🎧 18 You will hear a reporter who is talking about another tourist attraction in Brighton. You will hear the recording twice.

Listen and complete the table.

The Sewers – a tourist attraction in Brighton		
	location:	*underground*
a)	sewers are tunnels for …	
b)	were built in (year) …	
c)	were built to make Brighton …	safer and _____
d)	price for 12 year olds:	
e)	Who can't go?	children younger than _____

Part 3: Cricket in India ____ / 5

🎧 19 You will hear a radio interview about cricket in India. You will hear the interview twice.

Mark A, B or C.

a) The sport with the highest number of fans in the world is …

     A ☐ cricket.

     B ☐ basketball.

     C ☐ football.

b) In the 2015 Cricket World Cup the number of countries was …

     A ☐ 8.

     B ☐ 14.

     C ☐ 24.

c) Cricket has so many fans because the sport is …

     A ☐ very popular in India.

     B ☐ more interesting than basketball.

     C ☐ easy to learn.

d) The most successful cricket team comes from …

     A ☐ Australia.

     B ☐ India.

     C ☐ Europe.

e) People in other countries think that cricket …

   A ☐ is very exciting.

   B ☐ brings lots of money.

   C ☐ isn't very modern.

Part 4: St. Kilda   ____ / 5

20

You will hear part of a podcast about a very special group of islands in Britain. You will hear the podcast twice. What do the numbers mean for St. Kilda?

Write a letter, A–H, next to each number.

a) 100 ☐	A	seabirds
b) 1,000,000 ☐	B	people left on St. Kilda
c) 4,000 ☐	C	boats
	D	years of human history
d) 37 ☐	E	bags with letters
e) 1930 ☐	F	St. Kildans move to Scotland
	G	miles from Scotland
	H	sheep

B – Text-based tasks   25 pts

Part 1: Understanding signs   ____ / 5

> What information do these signs give you? Write down the correct letters.

a)

```
SLOW
SCHOOL
ZONE
```

A This is a school for slow learners.

B You have to drive slowly here.

C You mustn't run in the school.

b)

```
KNOCK AND WAIT
FOR PERMISSION
TO ENTER
```

A You have to apply for permission to get in.

B You can open the door after knocking.

C You can only go in if somebody calls you in.

c)

```
ALLERGY SAFE
LUNCH TABLE
```

A Only allergy-friendly food is eaten here.

B This table is reserved for kids without allergies.

C Stay away from this table if you have an allergy.

d)

```
THIS SCHOOL
OPERATES A STRICT
NO SMOKING
POLICY
```

A Nobody is allowed to smoke here.

B Teachers can tell you to stop smoking.

C You can smoke outside the school building.

e)

```
END
SCHOOL
SPEED
LIMIT
```

A Drive slowly on the last day of school.

B Speed limits in front of schools are illegal.

C You can drive at a normal speed.

Part 2 – Part 5: Text

> Read the following text carefully and carry out the tasks from parts 2, 3, 4 and 5.

The Mousetrap

Most plays and shows run for a few weeks, some for a few months. But when *The Mousetrap*, a murder mystery play by the famous English writer Agatha Christie, was put on stage for the 25,000th time in 2012, it had already been running for 60 years. And the play is still performed today, six days a week, with two shows on Tuesdays and Saturdays, making it the longest-running play in the world.

What's more, if you try to book, you may well find that you can't, because tickets have already sold out. For the fact is that this play has become a London attraction in its own right, just as much as watching the changing of the guards outside Buckingham Palace.

Agatha Christie actually wrote *The Mousetrap* as a radio play in 1947. But when it was first performed on stage, the theatre critics in many newspapers were not impressed. Agatha Christie herself predicted that it would run for a maximum of eight months. But the theatregoers proved them all wrong.

Of course, the actors in the play have changed over the years. One estimate is that more than 400 different actors have acted in *The Mousetrap* over the years. One actress, Natasha Rickman, actually played the very same role that her mother had played many years before – the part of Miss Casewell. Another actor, David Raven, is in the *Guinness Book of Records* as the longest performing actor ever – he played the role of Major Metcalf in 4,575 shows.

Of course, being a murder mystery, everybody wants to know who commits the crime: that, after all, is the point of the play. So given that over eleven million people have watched the play, you might think the surprise ending would by now be widely known. But at the end of every show, the members of the audience are asked not to reveal the secret or to share it on social media. And the impressive thing is that, by and large, the secret has been kept. Agatha Christie herself helped to keep the secret by making sure that the play has not been published as a book in the UK, and the play has never been made into a film.

Part 2   ____ / 5

> Match the letter of the headings with the correct number of the parts of the text.
>
> Write down the correct answers. Example: 6) – f)

1)	lines 1–9	**a)**	First reactions
2)	lines 10–15	**b)**	Cast members
3)	lines 16–22	**c)**	A world record
4)	lines 23–32	**d)**	So who did it?
5)	lines 33–46	**e)**	A tourist magnet

Part 3

_____ / 5

> Decide whether the statements are 'true', 'false' or 'not in the text'.
>
> Write down the correct answers. Example: f) – not in the text

a) The first stage performance of *The Mousetrap* was in 1952.

b) The tickets are very expensive because the play is so popular.

c) Everybody loved *The Mousetrap* from the beginning.

d) Natasha Rickman and her mother appeared on stage together.

e) Amazingly, most people don't know who the murderer is.

Part 4

_____ / 5

> Complete the sentences by choosing the correct ending according to the text.
>
> Write down the correct answers. Example: 6) – A)

1) *The Mousetrap* is special because it ...

   A is performed six days a week.

   B has been running for 60 years.

   C has been on stage for more than sixty years.

2) Most visitors to London ...

   A want to see the play.

   B prefer to see the changing of the guards.

   C have difficulties buying their tickets online.

3) Agatha Christie thought that ...

   A the actors weren't very good.

   B *The Mousetrap* wouldn't run very long.

   C the play would be very successful.

4) No actor or actress has ...

   A ever played the same role as one of their parents.

   B changed more than Natasha Rickman.

   C a higher number of performances than David Raven.

5) The name of the murderer ...

   A is known by millions of people.

   B isn't known by anybody.

   C is known by everybody.

Part 5

> Find the corresponding sentence parts or sentences in the text that mean the same and write them down.

a) As a result, *The Mousetrap* has been on stage longer than any other play.

b) It can be difficult to get in because all seats have already been reserved.

c) Journalists writing about the first theatre performance didn't like the play very much.

d) After each performance people are told not to talk about the identity of the killer.

e) It is amazing that on the whole people have kept quiet about the ending.

C – Use of language

15 pts

The Royal Pavilion in Brighton

Here I am in Brighton, _____a)_____ outside a strange, exotic-looking building, in a park with exotic trees and plants, with lots of towers, and five onion-shaped domes that don't look English at all. In fact, this building looks _____b)_____ a palace out of a child's book of fairy tales. Well, it is a palace – a real one. It was built between 1815 and 1822 for the son of the king of England, a prince called George. Prince George did not like working, and found London _____c)_____ serious. He preferred dancing and drinking and having expensive parties with his friends. So the palace, called the Royal Pavilion, was built to give Prince George a place _____d)_____ he could escape life in "boring" London. Today the palace is open to the public. You can walk through the living rooms, bedrooms, music rooms and dining hall of George and his rich friends, but also through the kitchens where the servants prepared the food and did the washing up. It's the contrast between these two lifestyles that _____e)_____ a visit so special. _____f)_____ fees are £12.30 for adults and £6.90 for children under 15.

Part 1

____/ 6

Read the text and find the correct word. Write down the correct word.

a)	staying	standing	spending
b)	how	as	like
c)	too	two	to
d)	who	how	where
e)	make	makes	made
f)	entrance	door	gate

Part 2

____/ 2

Find the opposites in the text. Write down the correct answer and the line.

a) daughter

b) cheap

Part 3

____/ 2

Find the synonyms in the text. Write down the correct answer and the line.

a) get away from

b) difference

Part 4 _____ / 2

> Choose **two** of the following words from the text and give a definition.

a) strange (line 3)

b) prefer (line 12)

c) kitchen (line 20)

Part 5 _____ / 3

> You want to know more about the Royal Pavilion. Ask **three** questions.

D – Writing 20 pts

Part 1 _____ / 8

> You want to work as a volunteer at a summer camp for children. Write an email and ask for information.
>
> Include **at least 3** of the following points:
>
> - where or when?
> - accommodation?
> - activities?
> - your skills or experience
>
> Write at least 60 words.

Part 2 _____ / 12

> Write about your favourite app. The following ideas can help you.
>
> | name? | why good? | advantages? | disadvantages? |
>
> **idea box**
>
> phone / tablet / watch / app store / download / buy / free / in-app purchase / communicate / play / learn / stream / share / save / ...
>
> Write about 80 words.

Prüfungsvorbereitung

- **Beginne rechtzeitig mit dem Lernen und mache dir einen Lernplan,** bei dem du auch Wiederholungsphasen einplanst. Starte mit Aufgaben, die dir im Unterricht noch schwerfallen. Hake ab, was du bereits erledigt hast.

- **Überlege dir, wo du im Englischen noch grundsätzliche Probleme oder Lücken hast** (z. B. Grammatikprobleme, die immer wieder auftreten). Diese Themen kannst du dann mit den interaktiven Übungen auf www.scook.de gezielt noch einmal wiederholen.

- **Mache dich mit dem Ablauf der Prüfung und mit allen Aufgabenformaten vertraut.** Plane im Vorfeld, wie viel Zeit du für jeden Prüfungsteil und für die Kontrolle zur Verfügung hast.

- **Schreibe dir auf, wann und wo die Prüfung stattfindet,** und plane etwas mehr Zeit für den Weg ein als sonst.

- **Lege alle Materialien am Vorabend der Prüfung bereit** (z. B. funktionstüchtige Stifte, Uhr; Smartphones sind nicht erlaubt!).

- **Achte auf ausreichend Schlaf und ein gutes Frühstück.** Wenn du dich gut vorbereitet hast, kannst du selbstbewusst in die Prüfung gehen!

Während der Prüfung

- **Behalte die Zeit im Blick!** Am besten legst du während der Prüfung eine Uhr auf den Tisch und schaust von Zeit zu Zeit darauf. Wenn du an einer Aufgabe festhängst, gehe lieber erstmal zur nächsten Frage weiter. Nimm dir am Ende einige Minuten Zeit, um deine Antworten noch einmal durchzugehen.

- **Lies die Aufgabenstellung gründlich durch,** bevor du mit der Bearbeitung beginnst. Manchmal enthält eine Aufgabe mehrere Teilaspekte. Markiere sie und übersetze sie dir zur Sicherheit in deine Muttersprache.

- **Nutze deine Chance!** Auch wenn du unsicher bist, ob die Lösung stimmt, so ist es ratsam, die Aufgabe trotzdem zu bearbeiten. So hast du zumindest eine Chance, dass es richtig ist. Kreuzt du keine Lösung an oder schreibst du keine Lösung auf, so bekommst du auf jeden Fall null Punkte. Kreuzt du aber mehr Lösungen an als gefordert, so verlierst du ebenfalls Punkte.

- **Mache dir bei Schreibaufgaben Notizen, wenn du gut in der Zeit liegst.** Sie können dir helfen, deine Gedanken zu ordnen und deinen Text sinnvoll zu strukturieren. Beachte aber, dass nur dein endgültiger Text in die Bewertung eingeht.

- **Gib deinen Texten eine gute Struktur mit Einleitung, Hauptteil und Schluss.** Beginne jeden neuen Textteil mit einem neuen Absatz. Halte dich an die geforderte Textlänge.

- **Formuliere klare Sätze.** Vermeide es, komplizierte deutsche Sätze wortwörtlich ins Englische zu übersetzen. Formuliere möglichst mit deinen eigenen Worten.

- **Kontrolliere am Ende,** was du geschrieben hast. Achte besonders auf Vollständigkeit, die Rechtschreibung, die Zeitformen deiner Verben und den Satzbau.

Wir wünschen dir viel Erfolg für deine Prüfung!